POWERLIFTING BASICS, TEXAS-STYLE:

The Adventures of Lope Delk

PAUL KELSO

IronMind® Enterprises, Inc.
Nevada City, CA 95959

Powerlifting Basics, Texas-style: The Adventures of Lope Delk
Copyright © 1996 Paul Kelso

Cataloging in Publication Data
Kelso, Paul—
Powerlifting basics, Texas-style
1. Weight lifting   2. Fitness and health   I. Title
1996   796.41   96-076289
ISBN 0-926888-04-8

Book and cover design by Tony Agpoon, San Francisco, California

Published in the United States of America
Ironmind® Enterprises, Inc., P. O. Box 1228, Nevada City, CA 95959

Printed in the U.S.A. First Edition
10 9 8 7 6 5

DEDICATION

For
the two red-headed 148-pounders in my life,
Jane and Lisa
White Lights

Other IronMind® Enterprises, Inc. publications:

SUPER SQUATS: How to Gain 30 Pounds of Muscle in 6 Weeks by Randall J. Strossen, Ph.D.
The Complete Keys to Progress by John McCallum, edited by Randall J. Strossen, Ph.D.
IronMind®: Stronger Minds, Stronger Bodies by Randall J. Strossen, Ph.D.
Mastery of Hand Strength by John Brookfield, foreword by Randall J. Strossen, Ph.D.
MILO: A Journal for Serious Strength Athletes, Randall J. Strossen, Ph.D., Publisher & Editor-in-Chief.

To order additional copies of *Powerlifting Basics, Texas-style*, or for a free catalog of IronMind Enterprises, Inc. publications and products, please contact:

IronMind® Enterprises, Inc.
P. O. Box 1228
Nevada City, CA 95959
Tel: (916) 265-6725
Fax: (916) 265-4876

CONTENTS

Introduction

Afterword

I sat in the trail hut near the top of the mountain, listening to the rain hit the corrugated metal roof. Mt. Fuji in Japan is far from the red clay country, but I was on familiar ground, talking powerlifting and weight training with a bunch of U.S. Navy men. One had a question.

"Aren't you that guy that used to write them stories about some college club in East Texas? You oughta' write a book about all that."

Well, yes, I am, and here it is.

Powerlifting Basics, Texas-style is directed at that great majority of people who want to train without depending on drugs or having to live in the gym. While not a beginner's "how-to" book, it contains straight talk for beginners, intermediates and just about everybody else who loves to slap on some iron for whatever reasons. There may not be much here for an advanced powerlifter in the last stages of contest preparation, and less for bodybuilding specialization, but there's a heck of a lot about how to get to those stages of your training career.

Veterans, old-timers and coaches will recognize situations I talk about and might share a laugh or two. Might get hacked off with me time or two as well. I'll tell stories about my old friends down in East Texas and the Wampus Cat Weight Club gang, put in a little history for the younger readers and lay out a few theories about trends in the Iron Game. You'll notice that I get a little testy about the peculiar notions that infiltrate weight rooms like terrorist elevator music.

Mike Lambert, publisher of *Powerlifting USA*, once wrote that I "write training fiction to make a point about training reality." Well, most of what I've written is 95% true. I've just changed some names and places to protect the innocent *and* the guilty. Much of the material in this book appeared in *PLUSA* in article form in the late 80's, and much is owed since to *PLUSA* and some to other magazines mentioned, but most is owed to the good men and women I've known in the game over the years.

When the Delk series ran in *PLUSA*, the response was worldwide. If I had had pictures of LaVonda Sue, I'd be rich today. Guys sent me their pics and letters to give to her! One guy wrote that he had driven back and forth on the Old Kilgore Highway (between Tyler and Kilgore) all night and never could find the Scoot 'N Boot. Another said he'd been in Nam with Lope and wanted his address. I got postcards asking when the Wampus Cats would lift next.

The East Texas characters and situations in *Powerlifting Basics, Texas-style* are creations of my imagination and bear no resemblance to any persons living, dead, or otherwise, or to genuine events or locales unless so identified or outright stolen for literary purposes. The figure of Lope Delk—I know him well—is based on a rugged but vanishing personality type whose loss to Texas and the American character I, for one, will regret.

Training methods are sketched out in the chapters.

In that time between trying to invent the Stretch Mark Machine and when I took off for Japan in July of '89, I helped the late Chester O. Teegarden keep his Strong Barbell Club in Sacramento going and assisted him in coaching a group of kids from the California Youth Authority who were more or less paroled out to us. Entered them in Olympic-style weightlifting meets in the Bay area. Chester's belief was that "all a kid needs is a good education and a barbell." I can't top that, and I wish it was printed on the masthead of every Iron Game publication in existence.

One of the questions pursued in this book is, "What is our purpose?" Far too many trainees seem to live in a semi-hysterical state in which they attempt every possible routine, ingest every mysterious and hopefully magical compound that comes along, and preserve their self-images at all costs from unpleasant suggestions or advice.

Why do any of us in the iron world do what we do?

Maybe it's the camaraderie of strength. Or the satisfaction of the senses from the smell and touch of wood and iron, chalk and leather, or the "whong" sounded when a big plate is loaded. Few will set world records or grace a magazine cover; all will benefit from sensible training. Is there any "high" better than a new personal record, or making real self-improvement?

Paul Kelso
Utsunomiya, Japan

POWERLIFTING BASICS, TEXAS-STYLE:

The Adventures of Lope Delk

PAUL KELSO

CHAPTER 1

How to Start a Training Club—and Live to Tell About It

"I don't need no weight liftin', Prof; I just wanna' get big."

I'm down under the bleachers in the Wampus Cat gym looking for the weight room, when this 138-lb. kid about seven feet tall, with a basketball under each arm, asks if I know where he can get steroids so's he can get "buffed up." I tell him the first thing we have to do is find the iron, then we'd talk.

I threw that "Prof" and the semi-colon in the opening sentence so you'd know I was an English teacher at Pine Woods Junior College in East Texas as of about two days prior to the above conversation. I had just finished three sections of freshman composition and wanted to get a workout. The kid opened a small door and waved me in before juking down to the office where the cheerleaders were licking envelopes for the coach's side insurance business.

I stepped into a concrete bunker about 10 by 12 feet and beheld the "modern" equipment the recruiting brochure bragged about. Modern in that it had been built in this century by the school maintenance man. In its entirety, we're talking about a leg extension machine operated by springs off an old Jowett cable set and a lay-flat leg press that could only be used by people over six feet tall. It was loaded with squares cut from steel beams left over from when the gym was built. These weighed from 42 to 57 pounds apiece, no two alike. The entire room was painted in the school colors: horse-apple and white.

I slid into Coach Bubba Koltuniak's office and stood there until he noticed there was somebody present who was not seven feet tall or wearing a cheerleader's skirt. Coach Bubba was the only man on campus who drove a pickup, chewed twist, and wore cowboy get-up complete with boots. He had come down from Pittsburgh years before and gone native in order to fit in and have a better shot at raising money from the Booster Club bankers. Coach Bubba and the bankers were the only people in the oil patch counties who still dressed that way.

I explained to the Coach how a lot of famous NBA players had gone to college as 138-lb. seven-footers and grown a couple inches and gained a hunnert pounds (yeah, I said that) by throwing weights around to a program that only I understood out of all the ironheads in East Texas. I told him if the Athletic Department, meaning him, would come off a few pesos, I'd build him a weight room for the team and I'd show 'em how to hold their mouths right and grunt on cue and in no time we'd be tough enough to stomp those rose-sniffers from Tyler J.C. Not to mention (which I didn't), I'd get to use the weight room at my leisure.

I found out later on that when the Coach started polishing his bald head when he was talking deal, it meant he held five aces and had the keys to your '55 Chevy in his pocket. He started shining his dome with a rag that looked like one of those chemical patches I used to carry in my trombone case back in junior high.

"Prof, I don't see why I couldn't let you have $5-600 to get rollin' and turn the whole thang over to you. Most profs don't take to the thump-ball program much, and I'm proud to place some of my boys in your history classes where I know you'll take special interest in them on court and off."

Well, I knew what he meant, but I sure thought I had him snookered because I was an English teacher, not history, and wouldn't have to pay off any favors.

The next day I had the money and two sections for men's and women's weight training added to my teaching load and was unofficial strength coach as a favor to the school Prez who appreciated my devotion to the students. I also discovered that the money had come out of student activities fees, which I was responsible for, being student council advisor, but the Coach would let the student body use the weight room when the team didn't need it. Seventeen guys weighing 138 lbs. stretched their seven-foot frames into desks in my English classes the following Monday.

I got the school one-ton and a couple of kids who knew what an Olympic bar was and cleaned out the basements of every barbell gym and fern-bar spa in a fifty-mile radius, took the stuff over to Lope Delk's welding shop and set him to work. My "bud" Lope is a little hard to figure. He's a loner, but knows everybody in four counties. I never found out just how many "bidnesses" he and his "cuzzins" owned or had a hand in around those parts. The man can be a tad dangerous to have as a friend, but I'd rather have him around in a crisis than anyone I know.

The cheerleaders and the "geek" fraternity painted over the school colors in the weight room and tacked some old York courses and pictures out of my scrapbook to the wall. The cheerleaders did it for school and team, and the geeks did it so they could get off that disciplinary probation they had picked up the year before for painting a deputy sheriff the school colors and roping him to the Confederate statue in the town square.

It didn't take but three six-packs to get the maintenance men to knock out a wall and relocate a four-by-six mirror out of the ladies' room in the Admin. building and hang it where some legitimate narcissists could get some use out of it. The ball team was hacked because we didn't hang the mirror the tall way, but the women students liked it as they could check to see if their leg warmers were properly rumpled.

In a month or so we had a pretty good weight room. The team got on the program and won the league championship two years in a row, mostly because they were heavier and stronger than their opponents and controlled the boards. I also taught a bunch of marginally literate guys to string a sentence or two together and got most of them through English on the square. Some flunked and Coach Bubba said not word one.

In late September of the second year, I drove over to the lake to see if I could scare up my English class amid the sea of student bodies stretched out on the sand beach at Lope Delk's Marina. They sure weren't in room 5B back in the Rod McKuen Fine Arts Center on campus. Some of the students hadn't been to class since Rush ended and several of us more dedicated teachers drove over there once a week or so to pass out papers and pick up assignments and make certain the cheerleaders were wearing their school color bikinis. Gave some of my best lectures and garnered some of my best insights under those conditions.

This big kid from Houston comes up with a keg under each arm and asks me since I used to compete in meets and wrote for the magazines and saw John Grimek tear the Chicago phone book in half when I was only six, how come I didn't take him and some other kids to a meet? I go back to my office and call Glen Venator in Dallas (he was regional director at the time) and ask if there are any Class III or college meets coming up where my kids won't get drubbed. He puts me in touch with Freeman King at Lamar U. down in Beaumont. King had a learning meet planned, said to come on down. We had eight weeks to get ready.

Later on I'll weave in some serious remarks about organizing a competitive training club and dealing with officials and administrators who aren't necessarily on your side, or worse, some that are. Meanwhile, getting it together for a powerlifting meet in eight weeks was SERIOUS.

I had a dozen prospects for powerlifting signed up in the club of maybe thirty. The school had 300-plus students—400 if you were the Prez talking to the trustees. Naturally there were quite a few who wanted to go into bodybuilding. I pointed out to them that the basics of both are nearly the same and that training for powerlifting would give them a good foundation for concentrating on bodybuilding later on.

I didn't have a chance of teaching the gang everything they needed to know, much less getting them on a training cycle when half of them didn't know what lifts were involved. I lined out a simple heavy and light for everybody and got on the phone. I called Venator for the rules, and Billy Jack Talton over at Louisiana Tech for the collegiate scoop, and half the ads in the back of *Powerlifting USA* for suits and wraps and DMG and 5000 liver tabs. I snuck the tabs onto the Coach's budget just to get even a little.

One of my very best lifters had a fondness for Neches River numbweed and complained that the B-12 in the liver tabs made him hyper. This kid needed some hyper so I doubled his dose. He stopped sleeping through breakfast and got on the training schedule and even made it to most of his classes. The school counselor thought I was a genius.

The Prez informed me there was no money to be had from any budget or campus fund to underwrite the club or the Beaumont trip. We countered with a car wash and a pancake supper and all those other high-tech fund raisers common to small town colleges. Raised $226.50 toward expenses.

As the word got out around as to what we were up to, "we" including some of the studliest men on campus, young scholars started coming out of the woodwork wanting to be in the club. This was partly out of boredom, partly curiosity, and a hair of pure scientific interest when several cheerleaders announced they were going to lift. The beehive brigade up in the registrar's office immediately went into overtime fluttering about the unsuitability of weightlifting for ladies. This was an Old South backwater, after all, and a couple of blue-haired dorm mothers complained to the Prez and to some of the girls' mothers that the fragile little things wouldn't be able to have children if they did such an unseemly thing.

Then the squat suits arrived.

Rule one when ordering suits as a club is to never trust the members to turn in accurate measurements. I had to be out of town for a few days and left a chart taped to my office door for the kids to write their measurements and weights on so Ernie Frantz's folks could sew 'em up right. I had posted the chart where the hourly between-class student stampede couldn't miss it. Naturally, all the boys listed their chest measurements too big and the girls recorded their waist and hip numbers too small. The weights for both sexes were a fantasy. You guessed it. I had to order fill-in sizes and even sent a couple of odd-shaped kids over to Longview for John Inzer to outfit.

The team meeting where we broke the suits out of the carton turned into a combi-nation rodeo and tag team match. People were struggling into and out of suits, wrangling over sizes and complaining. The blonde 121-pounder was concerned that her suit was too revealing. She was relieved, and the boys disappointed, when I told her it was O.K. to wear a T-shirt underneath. The other girls insisted on a closed try-on session with no men present. One wasn't seen in her suit until the meet. She had sewn a little skirt on it around the hips. Another girl's mom refused to allow her to wear her suit in public and told the Prez I had to be an immoral pervert. I heard later that my 132-lb. entry had worn her suit under her clothes for protection on a date with the campus Romeo. Might work. I actually had to defend the squat suits on moral as well as functional grounds at a faculty meeting. This was a church school, after all. In East Texas.

One student miss who was majoring in boys liked the way the suit fit so much she took to wearing it under a school-colors, skin-tight jump suit issued by the drill team for performances. She opened the thigh seams so her legs wouldn't fall off in the second half. When she went to her first meet at the Region Nine's in Austin, she sewed up the seams with ordinary thread. The suit blew out at the legs during her opening squat and she sat down on the platform and burst into tears. She got mad and put on another suit and came back to total.

One of the boys didn't bring his suit because he said it looked sissy and he could do better without it.

"I ain't wearing no ball-crusher suit."

This was the same hardhead who always forgot his USPF card, never brought any money on road trips, and trained his bench press four days a week. There's one, maybe two, in every club or gym. Usually they quit and spend the rest of their alleged careers telling everybody that the Coach is a jerk. I dropped him from the team but had to reinstate him when the school counselor told the Prez I was being beastly to the kid's psyche. Does this sound familiar?

We did make it to four meets that year. Won fourteen trophies against four-year schools and picked up a few in an Open. We got our pictures in the paper and made the ten o'clock news. Some of the students went on to larger schools and kept lifting. But the large meets we went to discouraged a number of the kids. It wasn't the competition, but the nonsense in the dressing rooms. The 148-lb. redhead decided to pack it in despite having the lifts to qualify for the Collegiate Nationals. She saw lady lifters smoking cigarettes and taking niacin, "bute" and speed between rounds. One well-known male lifter was rumored to have used cocaine at a big Open. Claimed it was the breakthrough he'd been looking for. It wasn't.

A competitor my 148-lb. redheaded women's entry had defeated by 75 lbs. in September leaped ahead by 125 in a Spring contest and had grown a pretty good mustache for a co-ed. A few Cat Club members drifted away. What had begun as an enthusiastic lark had gotten too serious for some. The club hardhead said he was going to continue, but somewhere else. He knew a "real" coach at a commercial gym who would put him on a "safe" steroid program. Right.

Don't be discouraged by the picture I've just painted about drug use. The events I described took place several years ago. The pendulum is swinging toward a lessening of drug use in weight sports, or at least tighter controls. Many meet-sponsoring organizations have imposed quite rigid testing. Drug free and "natural" lifting and bodybuilding groups are perhaps the fastest growing in the U.S. Also, a heck of a lot of people, athletes and coaches, are wising up to the dangers.

I've gotten a little off my subject, but if you're going to organize a club for competitors or one that includes them, you need to establish a policy or consensus about drug use at the outset. Drug free or not? Your club's stance will affect the makeup and even the size of the club and can determine success in acquiring and keeping sponsors. If a drug-user image, justified or not, blocks or prejudices chances for national TV sponsorship or entry into the Olympics, as it does for powerlifting, what are a local iron club's odds on getting corporate or institutional support close to home? Heck, I was under suspicion at the school for giving the kids liver tabs!

The only sponsors we had or could get was the school, which only ponied up traveling money after we had a few successes, and $4,500 over two years to build a $9,000 weight room, accomplished in large part because Coach Bubba and I were downright slick. Lope Delk "hepped" out regularly so we let him keep a couple trophies behind his bar at the Scoot 'N Boot roadhouse, and because he had his eye on my blonde 121-pounder. He also had a seven-foot, 250-lb. former Wampus Cat tending bar, putting things on the line:

"My man, how about easin' that change here in the jar for the weight lifters?"

Worked pretty well indeed, indeed.

Getting organized requires cooperation. One problem is a growing hostility between different competitive camps. Many powerlifters believe bodybuilders and weightlifters to be wimps, weightlifters often claim that they are true athletes and that bodybuilders and powerlifters are not, and bodybuilders prattle about their "superior lifestyle" and dismiss powerlifters as FAT and the weightlifters as having no pecs!

If we want our iron sports to grow, especially in our own backyards, we need to be mutually supportive. Even "mullets" must have a place to begin. That derisive term is used by an arrogant few "naturals" to whom gains came easy and by some personality-warped drug users to put down beginners and ordinary folk who want to train. That attitude is just not justified.

We were ALL mullets once except for a small group of the genetically blessed. My gang at the college were so green, they were IN the first meet they ever saw! Without the club they would not have shown up and without the support of a lot of decent men and women in the sport, they would not have continued.

Now let me tell you about some of the things that happened to the Wampus Cat Club and their friends, and about some of the things that couldn't happen, but did.

CHAPTER 2

The Bench Press and the Hardhead

I drove out the Old Kilgore highway and headed for Lope Delk's bar called the Scoot 'N Boot. When you ask a girl to two-step around those parts, it's "let's do some boot-scoot'n." Lope had phoned and told me to get over there as he had a great idea for raising money for the Wampus Cat Weight Club. This was a month after the powerlifters had got their feet wet at the "learners" meet at Lamar U. We'd all gotten excited and were fired up for the Region Nine USPF collegiates in a month or so, except that we were broke.

I pulled around back where the "patio beer garden" was set up. This consisted of four wooden phone-cable spools about two yards across, laid on their sides, and ringed by kegs and benches borrowed semi-permanently from nearby state parks. The whole thing was covered over by a barn-sized sheet of corrugated tin which had landed in the parking lot during the tornado of '83. Right in the center of the outdoor dance or fight floor was absolutely the biggest press bench ever constructed. Lope had welded it together out of nine-inch oil field pipe he had brought over from his junkyard in Seldom Seen, Texas, near where Floyd Lyons, the great Masters lifter, used to live. Maybe still does.

I figured this bench would support a combined weight of bar and lifter of maybe 9000 lbs. Lope's great idea was to stage bench press contests inside the "Boot" every couple weeks and split the proceeds with my school gang. Naturally, he expected the school to "hep" with publicity and encourage the club to show up and lift. This would do two things for him: bring in a lot more student business and put him into position to make moves on my blonde 121-pounder. Old Lope seemed to have forgotten that the church-affiliated school wasn't about to make an unholy alliance with him or any other honky-tonk operator, especially after that dormitory bootlegging incident with the fraternities and the cheerleaders a few years back.

Another small problem arose when he discovered that the bench was too big to get inside the building without knocking out an exterior wall. It's true that some rig-ape or tool-pusher could be counted on to drive his pickup through a wall at least once a year, but Lope wouldn't get an insurance payoff if he did it himself.

Delk is a pretty strong guy, having spent years in the oil fields and lumberjacking down in the Big Thicket woods as a young man. Stood just under six feet and weighed maybe 190. No fat. Now about all he did was bench press because of the gimp leg he got when a tree fell on him. Could bench about 340 with a bounce and a heave. Not bad for a 45-year-old guy who started late.

But I knew this was a snipe hunt or worse when I saw who else was under the roof nursing a pitcher apiece. None other than Coach Bubba Koltuniak and the club hardhead. They were in on this thing from the start. Lope was not only going to promote contests but *make* monster benches like the one in front of me. Coach Bubba would market 'em and the kid would pose for pictures and demonstrate.

This is the same kid I kicked out of the club and had to take back due to administration pressure more times than the town drunk had gotten saved at the revival tent. The boy's dad was a preacher. In the school's denomination. In East Texas.

The hardhead stated that Lope was now his coach. They could both out-bench me, which they thought proved that they knew more about training than I did. I pointed out to them that many athletes with great natural ability often turned out to be lousy coaches, because success had come relatively easy for them and they had never analyzed what it was that they were doing that made them great. In what other sport do so many trainees expect their coaches to out-perform them in order to establish credibility?

I looked at Coach Bubba. He never played organized basketball past the thirteenth grade, yet was one of the better junior college coaches in the country. I told Delk that his hero Ted Williams had sure been a top baseball star, but nobody elected him Manager of the Year in the big leagues. This attitude is a hardhead fallacy: that great ability indicates great knowledge. It can, but the Iron Game is full of people with this problem; many a *good* lifter or bodybuilder has failed to become *superior* because he wouldn't listen to anyone he could outlift or whose arms were smaller.

The kid is maybe 20 and I'm old enough to be his daddy. The kid looks at me and sneers.

"I've been liftin' since the eighth grade and you can't teach me nothin'."

"So have I," says I, "and you're probably right."

The remark sailed over the kid's head like a frisbee, but not Lope's. He backhanded the smirk off the kid's face and the boy did a gainer over a cable spool, not before Coach Bubba retrieved the pitcher off it, however. Lope tells the kid to mind his manners and asks me to set up a program for them and they would, by God, follow it.

"Well, let's see you guys do a workout like you always do it," I said.

You can guess what took place. They warmed up with 135 for 10 and then jumped to 205 for eight, grunted out 255 for five and heaved, bounced and flung their way up with singles and doubles and topped out around 305. Both swore they could do a lot more but had been drinking beer all day in celebration of their grand scheme. Right. I asked 'em how often they "trained." They owned up to two to three sessions a week, four when they were serious. It wasn't any use to ask about their regular day for training other body parts.

I'm not going to put quotes around what I lined out for them. Some of the language I used describing what I thought about their program might burn innocent ears. I could also see that Coach Bubba was losing interest in the whole thing; not only could he see that their brainstorm was sinking fast, he knew that the routines I had put the school ball team and lifters on worked, and Lope and the hardhead kid might as well be smoking Neches River Numbweed. Besides, there was no way to get that bench in his pickup. He split when I began presenting the facts of life.

Here's what I told 'em.

1) Train twice a week.

2) From your hand spacing and elbow rotation, I'd say you are both triceps pressers; you need pec and deltoid work and a wider hand spacing to shorten the distance the bar travels. One day a week, do flat bench DB presses, beginning with several light to moderate warm-up sets and the last three sets with reps in the five-to-seven range with constant weight. Follow this with two sets of close grip barbell benches with your thumbs right against your outer pecs. Eight reps. For instance, if you can bench 205 lbs. for a single, start with 125 or sixty percent. Once you learn the movement you can add weight quickly.

Finish with two sets of what I call the bench shrug, that is, raising and lowering the weight without bending the arms, by spreading the lats and rolling the shoulders up toward the bar, while contracting the pecs. This strengthens the shoulder girdle and develops the "shoulder roll" used by most great benchers, although many don't know they do it. Lower the bar again with straight arms, by pulling the shoulders down and in toward the bench and crunching the scapula together. Use a spotter on this one as the balance can get tricky, and because you will eventually be able to use huge weights after some practice.

Bench Press Training

Train bench twice a week.

First Day
1. **Flat bench DB press.** Two warm-up sets, 3 sets x 6-8 reps.
2. **Close grip bench press.** 2 x 8.
3. **Bench shrug.** 2 sets; begin with same weight as a 10-rep BP set and build up over several months while reducing reps to six over time.

Second Day
1. **Bench press with slightly wider grip than usual.** 3-4 x 8-10.
2. **Seated or high incline DB press, OR parallel bar dips.** 3-4 x 8-10. *Remember:* On every set of presses, pause at the bottom with the first one to two reps and then explode. (And do some real upper back work regularly!)

3) The second day, load the bar with about ninety percent of a weight you can normally bench for ten reps, for example, 135 lbs. if you can do 150. Set your grip *one finger wider* than normal. Maybe half a finger width. Practice with eight to ten reps for several weeks until you can do your previous poundage. Then scootch your grip out a hair again. You want to make triceps, pecs and delts share the load more or less equally. Of course, you don't want to go past the legal hand spacing width or past the point where you begin to seriously lose triceps power. Touch the bar at the highest point on your chest and begin with your elbows angled in toward your rib cage.

Yeah, yeah, I know bodybuilders often use an exaggerated wide grip lowered high on the chest with their elbows out to the side to make their pecs pretty and try to develop a pec-delt "tie-in." I don't think it's a good strength builder, and I do think it's a good way to wreck your shoulders.

Every time you move your grip wider, stay at three to four sets of eight to ten reps for a few workouts before trying heavier weights for six to eight. It ought to work out about a month or more at each hand spacing until you find the best position. Follow these with three to four sets, eight to ten reps of seated or high incline DB presses or weighted parallel bar dips, with elbows out about 45 degrees from the chest. You could do the DBs one week and the dips the next. Both in one workout may be too much.

4) *The most important thing:* Every set of bench presses on either day, lower the weight slowly and pause for a count of three on the first one or two reps of each set, drive it off your chest and then gun it along like your old hot-rod, gaining speed as it moves, faster and faster. Using this drive style with lighter weights (in the squat and deadlift as well) during practice will result in larger max attempts later on. Lope and the kid found that they had to use considerably less weight at first. You will too for a while before this type of program kicks in. I told 'em to stick to it until they could once again use the poundages they just demonstrated. Maybe three months. Then they should have a max-out day with contest rules. If their best single didn't take a big jump, I'd eat my squat suit with jalapeno sauce.

Then I had an afterthought. "Oh, and one other thing. Back work."

"Huh?"

"The great benchers have great backs. Thick lats."

The hardhead couldn't stand it. "Hey, man, gotta' get my pecs up more, anybody knows that."

Lope looked at me speculatively. I pushed on. "Humor me. Once a week, is that too much? Once a week do some high-pulls or power cleans, some bent over rows and some chins. A little balance, O.K.?"

The kid got out of range of Lope's backhand before he sneered, kinda hiding it from me this time as well. Lope considered me with a gaze that suggested that maybe, just maybe, I hadn't ridden into town on a wagonload of turnips.

The kid stuck it out two weeks and then went around bad-mouthing me because I had taken 50 lbs. off his bench and messed him up with the girls down at the Dairy Queen. Pretty soon he was back struttin' around, ego intact, and benching 330 like he was in the first place. Old Lope? He stuck it out and eventually benched close to 400 at 48 years of age. The blonde 121-pounder is still hanging around. Calls him "Uncle Delkie."

She didn't hang around because of his bench, but because of what she saw of his overall character and willpower—and she saw it was true of him not just in this situation, but as a man.

CHAPTER 3

Sin, Squats and Shakespeare

It was the afternoon of my birthday, February 6th, (me and Ronald Reagan), and I was discussing a squat suit order with my redheaded 148-pounder, when LaVonda Sue Braley announced that the Reverend Harley had come to see me. I know that's a heck of an opening sentence, but I thought I'd get into this disaster quick as I figured it would take me a while to get out.

I straightened up the office real fast and prepared for the worst. The good Reverend was a local gadfly who had taken on himself the mission of saving the area from rock 'n roll, drugs, communism, feminism, the Tri-Lateral commission, booze, humanism, jello hairdo's and the Democratic party. Not having made it on TV yet, he did not wear polyester suits or Ray Bans or have a sculpture-cut hairdo. His style was a cross between Colonel Sanders and Boss Hogg and he was built like a small college lineman imitating a Saturday night chicken-fried steak.

Brother Harley slammed a copy of the latest Weider mag on my desk.

"Sir, I demand to know who is paying you to infiltrate women's bodybuilding and posing briefs onto this campus in the guise of wholesome fellowship!?"

I told him the Weight Club had four women who competed in powerlifting, one thinking about bodybuilding, and the rest on trim-and-shape programs. Then he really got exercised, for him. He looked like he hadn't broken a sweat in ten years except for fighting his way back for seconds at church potlucks. But he was big, like a two-door refrigerator.

"Lifting! EVERYBODY," said he, "knows that women are not to presume on male domain! It's in the Book!"

He didn't mean one of Fred Hatfield's. He thundered that women are not supposed to assume male roles or attempt to compete in unnatural, for them, activities.

"Why if that sort of thing is allowed, high school girls will want to go out for football!"

(Note: The Texas education honchos ruled in early 1993 that women could no longer be barred from trying out for high school football, a catastrophe of biblical proportions for some of the old mossbacks.) I told him that there are national competitions for women and that some teams are sponsored by Christian organizations.

He couldn't take it. Collapsed in a chair by the door and stared at a picture of Bev Francis on the bulletin board. Then he noticed the redheaded 148-pounder, who was busy filing meet applications. Took a look out the door and into the outer office at LaVonda Sue (you were wondering, right?), busy playing secretary and munching liver tabs.

"Ain't she a cheerleader?"

He allowed as how that was a proper role for a young lady.

"Uh, Brother Harley, she trains with us," said I. "No meets yet, but she squatted one and three-quarters bodyweight last week."

To his eternal credit, the Rev looked me in the eye and admitted that perhaps things had changed a little since he played tackle for the Wampus Cats. Back when the school had a football team, that is. I "hepped" the old boy out of his chair and suggested we take a walk over to the field house where he could observe a club workout and assess the situation first hand. As we went out the door, he eyeballed LaVonda Sue.

"Ain't that the girl I seen over to Lope Delk's barroom the other night they had the bench contest?"

You'll recall Lope's bright idea about staging Saturday night bench-offs at the Scoot 'N Boot 'tonk out on the highway. That the Preacher Harley brought this up was my first inkling that his assault on the campus might turn out all right.

The Big Kid from Houston met us at the door of the weight room and asked if I'd heard about the "new" method of squat training he had picked up at a hard-core gym on his last home visit. Called it "puttin' on some wheels."

Seems the big guys there liked to get together and work up with 45-lb. plates. One hundred thirty-five to warm up; then 225, 315, 405, 495, and so forth. Strutted around saying stuff like, "I can do five wheels," and "If you can't do six, you ain't nothin'," and other homilies. That's plates on a side, of course. The Kid said he thought our gang ought to train that way. Five reps a set. Gonna' build up weight room camaraderie and weed out the riff-raff. I was just about to comment that such a program would weed out everybody on campus darn quick when the Reverend Harley brought the whole weight room congregation to attention with the following:

"The Bible speaks of preparing one's self in the ways of righteousness for the Lord's sake."

He went on to explain that there is nothing to be gained in life or weight training by allowing the arrogance of others to dictate one's preparations for one's calling. This elicited a mass "Huh?" from everybody in the weight room. The Rev looked at me.

"I, uh, used to work out in Dallas while I was in seminary."

He asked the Big Kid from Houston what his best single was and how long he'd been training. The answer was 474 max and two years on and off since high school weight work for football. The Reverend went into "kindly padre" gear.

"Look, son, you're maybe 19-20 years old. Why're you trying to keep up with guys who have been training for years, ain't ever competed yet and're worried more what their buddies think than they are in reaching their potential?"

I, like Br'er Rabbit, laid low. This was getting good. The Rev went on.

"I figure if you can do 474 once you can maybe do four to five at 380-90, in somethin' close to good style. If not, you are wasting the Lord's day and Coach Kelso's time."

He swung around to face the gang and stretched out his arms.

"Now hear me all you young people, trying every workout to lift maximum weight and to keep up with or best others is not only succumbing to avarice and envy, two of the Seven Deadly Sins of the Bible and weight training, it's just flat ignorant."

I about half expected him to pass the plate at this point.

"Now what you need to do, son, is stay under 400 'til you can do five reps right, and then go to 420 or so for a double or triple. Work it from there. Add weight. Add reps. It's in the Book."

The preacher was in kind of a trance at this juncture. The Kid looked like he'd been drilled between the eyes by an ivory- billed woodpecker. (I know they're extinct, but I swear I saw one back in '87.)

Brother Harley loosened his string tie and continued.

"After that, drop back to 315 and grind out 15-20 reps. If you can't, take off some more weight. Forget trying to max for three, four months."

He was standing wrong way behind a preacher curl bench by this time, using it as a pulpit. I knew the organ music I heard was from the chapel across the way. Wasn't it?

"I shall close now by saying that you should forget about 45- and 100-pound plates when what you need are 5's, 10's and 25's. It is better to succeed with a pair of two-and-a-halfs than to fail with 45's for thy ego's sake. Remember, as it says in the Bible about bein' true to your own self and it follows as the night the day that thou canst not be false to any man . . ."

He sort of petered out at this. What had I just heard? Old Testament? Shakespeare? I can hear old Hamlet now, "To bench or not to bench . . ."

The Preacher had never heard of percentages for setting up training loads. He thought Dr. Squat was a pro-wrestler and *PLUSA* was a subversive organization. May be. But somewhere along the way he had picked up some good advice. Train and live within your capabilities, and be true to your own potential. That ain't bad. I oughta' put out a T-shirt with that device.

Brother Harley hung around the gym for an hour or so. Eventually he got up and coached some beginners on how to hold their mouths right when backing out for a squat. He watched the interaction between the men and women lifters and felt their mutual sense of purpose. As we walked to his car he "owned up."

Preacher Harley's Training

Work sets of 80-85%. Many top lifters recommend 5 x 5 or even 8 x 3 in the middle six to seven weeks of their training cycle, stopping four to six weeks before a contest and changing to sets of fives, threes and twos. If not contest cycling, finish the workout with a drop-back set for reps with 60-65%.

"This day has been instructional for me. I've been so busy tilting at windmills the last few years that I've forgotten about aspiring to greater heights. I've been flailing at straw men and not dealing with real men. And women."

A few months later he took a position with a Bible college over near Henderson and talked 'em into ordering a couple thousand dollars worth of iron and started a local chapter of one of the Christian athletes' associations. We weren't on the same wavelength theologically; I've got my weaknesses and he his, as you'll find out. But we became good friends. Besides, I wanted to find out about the other five Deadly Sins of weight training.

Preacher Harley gets a mite confused. The classical Seven Deadly Sins are not from the Bible *or* Shakespeare. They're from the works of that great Italian lifter, Dante. Maybe you remember him from sophomore Lit. In descending order of importance, the Sins are Pride, Envy, Anger, Sloth, Avarice, Gluttony and Lust. There's something in each of Dante's sins, and Preacher Harley's definitions, to consider as we progress.

The Seven Deadly Sins

1. **Pride.** Buying a tank top and strutting after three months' training.
2. **Envy.** Changing programs every month trying to copy your latest hero.
3. **Anger.** Rebelling against your coach and thinking you know more than he does 'cause you can out-bench him.
4. **Sloth.** Thinking training is more important than your education or career.
5. **Avarice.** Trying to find out how much you can do before you know what you are doing.
6. **Gluttony.** Trying every new supplement and wonder drug that comes along.
7. **Lust.** Thinking big muscles are all you need to score with the opposite sex.

CHAPTER 4

Call Me Old-fashioned

I'm in my office up in the classroom building one day going through a stack of what Ken Leistner's mailman used to call "comic books" (glossy bodybuilding magazines), when the Big Kid from Houston eases in with a problem. Says he wants to lift in the Ark-La-Tex meet in the spring and train for football at the same time, as he plans to transfer to the four-year school at Nacogdoches in the fall.

He complained that he couldn't get a good workout in our weight room because the equipment was too old-fashioned. No pec-dec, no cable crossover, no leg sled, hack machine or seated calf raise; no nothing. All we had in the early days was a squat rack, a bench, a couple Olympic sets, one power bar and a lot of loose dumbbell bars and plates. This guy had a build like a black panther and the sleekness of a seal. Weighed about 200 at 6'. Benched 280, squatted well but was behind on the deadlift and other big pulling movements. If he did them at all.

I explained the programs I had the Wampus Cat powerlifters and round-ballers on and suggested a few football-oriented changes.

"I know about that stuff, I want to use modern methods and show up *buff*," he said.

I could see we had a little translation problem.

"Did you ever hear of Charles A. Smith?"

"Who?"

"Lived down in Austin. Wrote for Joe Weider for years. He used to say, 'There is nothing new in weight training.'"

The Houston Kid looked at me like I had just spoken to him in Chinese. He picked up one of the "comic books" and pointed out a picture of the current pro "Mr. Sensational" as his goal. Besides, he didn't care much for squats that much as they hurt his shoulders. I caught on as to what I had here. Another young trainee who confused appearance with ability. (There is no true correlation between size and appearance with strength and ability.) Then he said he'd like to look so good when he got to the college that the football coach would come up to him and ask him to try out.

"You must have been watchin' old Mickey Rooney college movies," says I. His expression was blank.

It is really sad that so many have no conception of what it means to be able to actually DO something, and what it takes to accomplish goals with reasonable expectation of success. These fantasies are encouraged by the tendency of some publishers and writers in the game to market image instead of the acquisition of competence. Miss a workout? Take a pill. Paint on some bottled suntan and buy a cantilevered shirt and go struttin' with your earphones on. Heck, I just wrote a song!

I told him that the first thing he was gonna' do was go back to the dorm and write a letter to the coach and tell him that the Houston Kid wanted to play football for him, what position he wanted to try and ask what weight he should come in at. The second thing was to pay up his power club dues and I'd send off his entry for the spring contest four months hence. The Kid's expression slid over toward panic. The third thing was to meet me in the weight room at four o'clock. He made a sound like "homina-homina" and blurted out that he needed time to think about it.

Then I caught on. He was using me as a sounding board to find out if his dream had any plausibility. Maybe he would have been relieved if I'd told him to forget it, I don't know. I decided to act like a professional educator and molder of youth instead of a professional curmudgeon.

"Look, you've been studying this. I think you've got a shot. It's a long time 'til fall. Come on down to the gym at four and we'll get started."

He stumbled out.

I sat there a few minutes longer and read in one of the "comic books" about a student at a Big Ten school who got a Master's degree for proving that three sets of eight to ten reps with eight or nine basic exercises is a more effective way to train than one set each of twenty or so various movements. Where did I first read that, *Strength & Health* in 1949? Peary Rader's *Master Course*? Then I saw in a coaches' mag that a kinesiology major had proved that excessive stretching before competition reduced power and performance. I had heard that from MacAdoo Keaton, the famous SMU track coach, back in 1955. He helped Jack Adkisson (later known as pro-wrestler Fritz Von Erich) to become the number two college discus thrower, and Forrest Gregg (later All-Pro with the Green Bay Packers) to throw the javelin from here to Fort Worth.

There was more. A 1992 study proved that vitamin-mineral and amino supplements were unnecessary for athletes if they ingested a well-balanced diet in sufficient quantities. Right. How about somebody developing a sure-fire program to guarantee that the athletes will eat such a diet? Good luck.

Another article quoted a Ph.D. strength coach as saying that trainees should not follow programs based on anecdotal evidence until they'd been tested under academic, scientific conditions. Translated, that means that 80 years of reports in non-academic books and magazines in the field are questionable. Yes, there has been a lot of baloney. But are methods that were proven or disproven in training or by trial in competition to be dismissed as *anecdotal*?

Certainly the game needs the benefit of sound research and new scientific exploration. However, it is my opinion that we are just reaching the point in the growth of our game where we are beginning to understand what the questions are. Please remember that academic study of weight training did not really begin until the mid-fifties, and then in the face of hostile opposition, with the boom taking off in the '70s. And, in contrast, that the first realistic world championship in weightlifting was in 1889. Surely there were valuable insights during the interim period.

May I suggest that before spending a lot of money and wasting students' time that the new breed of academics in weight training and competition familiarize themselves with the history of this activity, consult with the aging old-timers still involved, and peruse the "anecdotal" literature? They could save themselves the risk and embarrassment of telling a lot of people what they already know.

Yeah, I know. Maybe I am a curmudgeon.

The Houston Kid wanted modern? I'd give him modern. I just had to get some "new" equipment. I went down to the campus shop and got a couple of tow chains. Then I drove over to Lope Delk's construction yard and "borrowed" one of those big hooks they attach to crane cables to swing wrecking balls from. I couldn't get the wrecking ball in the car. Just as well.

I met the Kid in the weight room on time. He was wearing posing trunks and pretending he didn't see me while he did some alternate DB curls. I was supposed to be all agog at how "buffed" he was. He had done that peculiar psychological twist common to the young (and some older folks who are allegedly grown up) of challenging me to make him do what he wanted to do in the first place.

True, he did have an impressive visual physique. Sort of early gymnast: bulbous pecs, biceps like softballs, high lats and carved-out lumps above the knees. It was obvious how he had trained up to that point: for the beach. He could carry pony kegs of beer pretty good.

The Kid pouts, "O.K., Coach, I'll try it your way. Now what's this super program I'm gonna' do?"

I exhaled slowly, under control.

"First throw these two chains over the rafters so the ends hang down on each side, then take that hook over to the parallel bars."

The Kid looks at me like I'm crazy. He takes care of it, nearly knocking himself silly when the chains whipped around. I admit I had mixed feelings just then.

Then I put him through a few tests. He couldn't deadlift much more than he could bench, which is far too common, didn't know what a hook grip was, and thought a shrug was a Padre Island shore bird. I worked him up on jerks off the rack and had him hold each one for a count of five. By the time he got to 185 lbs., he was shaking like that guy on the space roller coaster in the movie "2001."

"What we are gonna' do, Kid, is work you in ways and from angles you never imagined. You'll end up with more overall strength and maybe some increase in athletic ability. You're also gonna' have a back from the planet Mongo. Here's the program, and it isn't modern."

1) Standing DB presses—1 x 8, 3 x 6. Heels together. Improves pure pressing power while increasing control and balance.

2) Overhead supports—3 single reps, each held overhead for five seconds. The bar is suspended in the chains (you can use a power rack) almost to full lockout over your head. Get under the bar and use your legs and arms to lock it out at full extension over your head, like finishing a jerk. Bring your feet in line. Stabilize under it and hold it for the count. Control the weight and work to your limit. I hope I'm not confusing anybody by mentioning the jerk. Weightlifting—Olympic style—remember?

3) Dips—When you can do 4 x 10, start using a weighted belt and go for six to eight. Our hook is 50 lbs.; when you can start hanging DB's on that, you are getting to be somebody. Perform these with the elbows held back at about 45 degrees and try to find a position that involves the delts, pecs, triceps, lats and serratus more or less equally. Dips have been called "the upper body squat," and are extremely useful in a limited program. They should be practiced regularly by anyone wanting strength along with development.*

4) Power cleans from the floor—4 x 5. Jerk the first rep of each set. With the bar on the floor, start the lift with the legs and then pull with the back and arms, rising to full body extension. Do not split the legs forward and back. Dip the knees slightly to help get the shoulders under the bar as you rack it in. Get someone to show you if you don't know how. This very basic movement will do wonders for your pulling power and develop columns of muscle from your heels to the base of your skull. Do the first two sets with moderate loads and think speed, and then add weight for the last two sets. Caution: don't throw the bar; pull it straight up. Please treat this movement as an exercise and not as a lift. Add small plates every workout if you can, and the poundages will mount over time.

The Big Kid's Training

1. **Standing DB press.** Heels together. 1 x 8, 3 x 6.
2. **Overhead supports.** 3 x 1. Each rep held five seconds.
3. **Parallel bar dips.** 4 x 10. With weight belt, 4 x 6-8.
4. **Power cleans from floor.** 4 x 5.
5. **Squats.** 1 x 10-12, 3 x 8; squat step-out: 3 x 1.
6. **Kelso shrug.** 3 x 10.

Every *third* workout: Do *only* squat and bench, 4 x 6-8, and deadlifts, 4 x 5; first and second sets with moderate weight, then two work sets. Alternate exercise: bent-arm pullover and press instead of dips. If splitting the routine, include it one day and do dips the other.

*Arthur Jones proposed the bent-arm pullover as the upper body squat. I included it in The Kelso Bone Structure and Growth Course published in 1980, calling for its comeback. I believe that the bent-arm pullover and press is due for a revival as a prime exercise in any abbreviated program.

5) Squats—After a warm-up set, grind out three sets of eight with a weight you can handle in good form, high-bar style. Then drop the weight down by a third and go for one set of maximum repetitions. The most important thing: on the first rep of every set, try to shrug the weight upwards with your shoulder girdle. This is the old Hise shrug and it will accustom you to heavy loads faster than anything I know about. Every two weeks or so, load the bar with about 95% of your best high-bar single and simply back out of the racks and set up. Try to shrug the bar a few times, and then put it back. Do this three times. Use spotters, or live—maybe—to regret it.

6) Kelso Shrug—3 x 10. Perform on a low-angle incline bench, under 45 degrees, lying face down. A curl grip on the bar, lifting straps until your grip catches up and big iron are the ticket. Shrug the bar up toward the chest, concentrating on a point in the middle of the upper back, not up toward the ears. "Yeah, but ain't that modern," you ask? Maybe, maybe not. The shoulder girdle has been able to "shrug" to the rear since it was invented. Vary your hand spacing and grip set-to-set for different "feels."

There's a reason for my including the weightlifting moves. I love 'em. I started as an Olympic-style weightlifter back when there was no such a thing as powerlifting. It is a terrific high to succeed with personal record overhead lifts, when everything is perfect and in the groove. I think every weight trainer should try a long cycle on the lifts at some point in the first several years of training. It'll help with whatever you decide to do with the iron in the future and make you strong and quick. But there is a danger; you might get hooked!

For three months the Kid did each of these movements once or twice a week, splitting the program in several combinations at first because it was just too much to do them all in one session when he began. Probably started too heavy, which was my fault, not his. Every third workout was competition-style squat, bench and deadlift, nothing else, 4 x 6-8. One month before the meet we went to lifts only, three sets of work sets of three to five reps after a few warm-up sets.

His personal record total jumped 100 lbs. at the contest. He came back to the "old-fashioned" program after the Ark-La-Tex and gained fifteen pounds by the time football season rolled around. He made the team at the four-year school and earned a letter his senior year.

Is there a moral to this story? How about this: Dreams can be realized if you are willing to take the risk of failing.

CHAPTER 5

A Burning Issue

I just want all you folks who are building a list of excuses to get out of workouts, and squats in particular, to know that I discovered a beauty a few years back. I was boiling cowboy coffee on the old wood burner in the fishing cabin that me, Lope Delk and Preacher Harley went in on three ways to use as a hideout from students, bill collectors and marriage-minded choir directors respectively. I was cleaning up from the breakfast of fried chicken (skinless, no batter) basted with peach preserves (not jam, not jelly), grits, biscuits, gravy, slices of cold, local tomatoes as big as softballs, and those wonderful sweet white onions they grow west of Tyler that you can eat like an apple. You can fish or work all day on that.

The Preacher was meditating—that is—flat out asleep on the porch, and the dog was under the card table studying how to retrieve the plate of leftover chicken from the sideboard. This mutt was a purebred lunch hound, who had adopted us and dropped by to help us with dinner whenever he could. He had the body of a Labrador and the legs of a dachshund. Lope had named him Squatlo. Do I have to explain that?

Then Lope busted into this tranquility and flogged a six-pound black bass down on the table.

"In case you haven't noticed, Kelso, that is a semi-good fish! Aahyawhyoo!"

Well, what with the bull roar of an East Texas good ole' boy and the feel of forty-year-old oilcloth on his scales, that old Hogmouth did a back one-and-a-half about four feet up and out and slapped the tin coffee pot straight up in the air and dumped a quart of scalding chicory and branch water into my shorts.

Imagine my surprise. Imagine my response.

I set the all-time land speed record for clearing the porch, did a perfect western roll over a drying minnow net, shucked my shorts in mid-air and managed a thirty-foot long jump that Carl Lewis would die for into the lake, swamping a rubber float full of cheerleaders from the school (we made a few exceptions).

I pulled up on the raft and considered how a guy could go about dying voluntarily. LaVonda Sue Braley, my secretary and 132-pounder, gazed upon me with 10,000-year-old eyes.

"Mr. Kelso, that sure is an interesting hickey you have there."

The "hickey" she referred to was a blister the height and circumference of a ten-pound plate. It was located just inside my hip bone. It was close and I don't mean as in horseshoes and hand grenades—I mean close! As Lope and Preacher Harley loaded me into the truck, I heard several irreverent giggles concerning the condition of my obliques. I made an oblique reference under my breath concerning their lineage and personal preferences. The Preacher looked straight ahead as we clanked off with me draped over the splash boards making noises like a beached mudtom.

The doctor's office was in a building Lope owned and referred to as The Croakery. Housed a chiropractor and a dentist as well as the doc. This was the entire medical corps for the county west of Cooney, Texas. Doc Culpepper cleaned up the blister, busted by then, and dressed it. Then he poked around on me, listened here, thumped there and made me cough a few times, which ain't much fun when sporting a nine-inch circle of raw meat on your nether parts. Weighed and measured me for the record.

The doc stared at me for a minute. Then he looked at Lope and Preacher Harley out in the waiting room. "I don't wish to presume, sir," he began, and then proceeded to presume all over the place. The gist of it was that he was not accustomed to treating naked patients wrapped in horse blankets. Further, he stated that it was apparent to him that I and my companions were overage and overweight for the type of shenanigans that produce such calamities as I was sporting. What he thought we'd been up to, I couldn't say.

Then he took a look at a height/weight chart on the wall supplied him by an insurance company in 1973, and announced that my ideal weight for my height and age was 185 pounds. I'm 6'2" and 226 at the time and had lifted in a Master's two weeks earlier. The doc stood maybe 5'9" and foundered in about 260. Looked like Alfred Hitchcock with glasses. The vein pattern in his nose resembled a street map of downtown Waco.

I was explaining to the doc who I was and that I still worked out and competed sometimes and that I was strength coach for the Wampus Cats over to the college when Lope straggled in.

"Kelso, you dead yet?"

"Do I look dead to you?"

Lope pulled off his hat and ran a hand through his hair, playing it for all it was worth.

"Hard to tell about you sometimes."

Lope and I gave each other the hairy eyeball until the doc got good and nervous, then I turned and asked him if he had ever heard about measuring the percentages of lean muscle mass as opposed to fat as an indication of fitness. Nothing.

He then said we were crazy to lift heavy at our age because of heart strain, arthritis, spinal damage and other no-no's. Does this sound familiar? Lope told the Doc not to worry as I wouldn't be doing any deadlifts for a while with that chancre on my belly.

"Deadlifts? You men do *deadlifts*? My son's been trying to learn those but can't seem to get anywhere."

Lope and I were caught. No way out. Sigh . . .

"What's the problem?"

Out of the corner of my eye I saw Brother Harley ease into the American Legion Hall across the street. Got while he could.

It's no surprise what we heard. The same old litany. The boy got with his friends and tried to have a contest every workout. Then they found a magazine featuring an article about advanced competitors. The kids were pulling doubles and singles and trying sumo style and getting hurt every other session.

I asked if the boy was doing a complete basic program, especially squats. Doc was shocked.

"Why, no. The football coach told 'em not to squat, says he read an article by some fellow at A&M said they were bad for the knees."

I'd read the same article. Published over thirty years ago and still rattling around in the iron world after all these years like a runaway computer virus. Both squats and the guy who wrote it got a bad rap when the article came out, as just about everybody misinterpreted the conclusions.

I asked the Doc if his kid was gonna' play football. Doc allowed the boy was too small and already a high school senior, anyway. I made some notes on the doc's prescription pad and handed it to him. "Well, maybe we can make him into a lifter. Have him do these for three or four months and then come see me."

The note read this way:

Two or three workouts a week. One day do the first group of exercises and the next workout do the second group. Then repeat the first group the following workout and so on.

The first group, do four sets of eight of behind neck presses, power-style squats, and bench press, and three sets of six of power cleans. The second day open with four sets of six reps in the deadlift using the standard style, hands outside the knees, feet under the arm pits or closer, head up, butt down. No sumo style. Keep the back flat and the arms straight, and pull. Try to push the floor out from under you. (I didn't get all that on one prescription sheet; I told the doc a lot of it as I wrote.)

After a five minute break, do two sets of squats for 12 reps, high-bar style. Finish up with three sets, eight to ten reps of flat bench dumbbell presses, bent over rows and either triceps extensions or close-grip bench presses with your hands 15-18 inches apart. If you have any energy left on either day, you can do one or two sets of curls and calf raises. You can do leg raises, situps and ab crunches at home on off days while watching the tube.

Basic Training

Train two to three times a week. Alternate the workouts.

First Day
1. **Behind the neck press.** 4 x 8.
2. **Power-style squats.** 4 x 8.
3. **Bench press.** 4 x 8.
4. **Power cleans.** 3 x 6.

Second Day
1. **Regular deadlift.** 4 x 6. Five minute break.
2. **High bar squats.** 2 x 12.
3. **Flat bench DB press.** 3 x 8-10.
4. **Bent-over rows.** 3 x 8-10.
5. **Triceps press on bench, OR close grip bench press.** 3 x 8-10.

Both Days
One to two sets of curls and calf raises. Do leg raises and ab crunches at home on off days two to three times a week.

"Doc, it wouldn't hurt you to work out with the kid. Do the same routine, but with a lot less weight, fewer sets and more reps. Spend a little less time on that bar stool out to the golf course."

He drew himself up to his full height and withered me with a haughty reply: "Sir, I pursue a skill sport."

Right. In a golf cart. Sand greens.

And that, dear friends, is how I ended up walking down Main Street wearing a diaper and doing a passable Gandhi imitation. We scooped Brother Harley out of the Legion before he could finish his third Nehi (into which he had snuck a little "supplement"), and headed for the cabin. Lope and the Reverend called me "Mahatma" off and on for the best part of a year until Doc Culpepper's kid got his Class III badge in his first meet.

A little respect, please.

CHAPTER 6

Dear Mr. Kelso: What Should I Do?

Coach Bubba Koltuniak slid in and plopped down a stack of mail about a foot high on my desk.

"Looks like you been doin' a little mail order on the side, Kelso. Better not be usin' Wampus Cat stamps."

This from a guy who was operating a side insurance business out of his office, but then, he had won the basketball league championship the year before. How he had convinced the cheerleaders that it was part of their duty to the school to stuff envelopes for him, I hadn't figured out.

"What do all those people write to you about, anyway? You got one here from Calcutta. Ain't that down by Houston?"

I told the coach to knock off the corn pone act. I wasn't gonna' contribute to the Booster Club and I wasn't gonna' buy insurance. He came down from Pennsylvania years ago and had gone native so bad that he was beginning to think he was a descendant of Alamo veterans instead of Polish steelworkers.

"Coach, most of these are from young guys who want to be big and strong without having to work for it. They think I've got some magic method that'll do it by next week."

Coach pulled off his rain-creased cowboy hat and rubbed his bald head.

"Sounds like some of my B-ball hot-shots. Gonna' go straight to the NBA without doin' drill or playin' dee-fense."

He wandered out, stopping to lean over my secretary's desk and give her a big gum-chomping leer.

"Howdy, LaVonda, you been giving any thought about me fixin' you up with that scholarship down to the University? Whyn't we take a drive and talk about it some?"

Miss Braley, my 132-pounder, studied him with her ancient wisdom eyes and quietly replied that she had decided to enter a religious order.

"I want to be the first flexing nun."

We managed not to start snickering until Coach disappeared into the library where he would try his charm on Miss Stotts. This is the lady who called me up every month to snuffily inform me that "those publications you ordered are here again!" This had been going on for a year or so. Miss Stotts was one of those cute sixties look-alikes with the granny glasses. Her main regret in life was that she was born too late for that scene. She made up for it by being about the only woman in town into New Age and feminist pro-grams.

She regarded *Powerlifting USA* as evidence of "insecure male overcompensation." Sounds like another good T-shirt slogan. She shrugged off *IRONMAN* as "an anti-intellec-tual expression of narcissistic testosterone poisoning" until John Balik took over and started putting nekkid ladies on the cover. Then her remarks took on a *serious tone*. Miss Stotts secretly liked old Coach, however—thought he was a salvage prospect.

I dug into the pile of letters to see what, or whom, I could salvage. The first guy wanted to know why he couldn't gain weight. He wanted to become enormously bulky and bench 600. The program he was on would put Ken Lain, Arnold and Hulk Hogan in the hospital. Eight or nine exercises totaling 40-50 sets of bench presses and assistance work. Said he did "bodybuilding stuff" for his legs and back 'cause he wanted to get his bench up first.

The next guy said he was a beginner. He started training with some kind of a two-workouts-a-day, five-days-a-week program that needed a computer to keep straight. He stuck to it for six weeks, got injured and was wondering what went wrong.

I was about to round-file the whole lot when a fellow name of Dell knocked on the door jamb. He ran a bait shop and boat rental place down on Lake Sam Rayburn with his daddy. I'd fished out of there and talked iron with him a few times. Dell was a small-boned man of 24 who had been training at a fern-bar spa since high school. He was in hard shape, wiry and tight, and weighed 175 at 5'10". Not bad at all, especially for a guy with interests other than Iron Game competition. Just fine the way he was.

Except that's not what he wanted.

You guessed it.

Dell had met one of the top pro "Mr. Sensational" contenders at a seminar in Houston a few months earlier. The bodybuilder told Dell that he knew the perfect steroid stack prescription to make a champion of a fellow with Dell's physique and that he, former "Mr. Wonderful," would supply 'em to Dell at wholesale out of the goodness of his heart. Yaazz, indeed.

What Dell wanted from me, now that he had a six months' supply of Deca, Anavar and horse 'roids, was to write him a training routine that would *go best with the drugs!!!*

"I been reading your stuff in the mags, man, and I just know you're right to fix me up's why I drove on up here."

I stared at him in awe and disbelief.

"Dell, I do believe you've got things turned a hair bass-ackwards. You been training five years pretty much steady and if you've been trying to get a competition body and you're still 5'10" and 175 then you've been doing something WRONG. How the heck have you trained up to now?"

He told me about it. Following the spa's program at first, then trying sure-fire methods suggested by other fellows in the gym. Changing his routine with every new issue of this magazine or that, trying to incorporate the alleged secret programs of the champions into his own. Never sticking to any one program long enough to give it a chance to work, but still managing to overtrain. Does this sound familiar?

I laid it out for him. Old Kelso has a couple rules that need to be confronted more or less in sequence:

1) You have to make up your mind what you want from training. Image? Competition strength or bodybuilding shape? Weight gain or loss? General fitness? Enhanced athletic ability? There is nothing wrong with any of those goals and they often complement each other. Do you want to hang around the drive-in hamburger joint or the honky-tonk being impressive, or enter contests? Both? The answer to the above determines the exercise and nutrition program you choose, not the choice of the spa employee with his or her own agenda or the second-hand opinion of the jerk at the gym with the legendary cousin who benches 700 in his basement.

2) You must try to reach your natural potential before you even think of drugs, 'cause that's what they are. A couple years basic, progressive training will allow you to analyze how far you may go in the game. Whatever your decision about continuing, you will have made permanent, safe improvement with lifetime benefits, whether you have the potential to become a champion or not.

3) You cannot hope to succeed with advanced routines until you have spent enough time in basic training. A rule of thumb for that might be when you can do a double bodyweight squat and deadlift and a one-and-a-half times bodyweight bench *for reps* for powerlifters, or a one-and-a-half times clean and jerk for weightlifters. (Bodybuilding is hard to measure: maybe it's when your growth plateaus without drugs or when you think you are big enough and need to concentrate on balance among the parts, definition and other considerations.)

If you don't understand and agree with those three rules, then Miss Stotts was right about you. You are training for the wrong reasons.

Do basic bodybuilding for the first six months or so before attempting any style of competition lift. Not to be confused with contest bodybuilding, this is a foundation for all iron sports and strength training. Work up to three to four sets of six to ten reps for upper body moves, and eight to fifteen reps for lower body, drawn from eight or nine exercises such as squat, bench, military press, deadlifts, power cleans or high pulls, bent over rows or chins, curls, calves and waist work. I have listed these in the order of my personal preference for gaining both size and strength, with the first movement first.

1. **Regular squat, high-bar style.** No board under heels unless needed for balance: power-style, trap bar on platform, low starts in power rack. Front squat or hip belt for extra quad work.

2. **Regular bench press,** flat or incline close grip BP, DB bench press, parallel bar dips. Bent-arm pullover and press are great in a bulk program.

3. **Overhead press**, military or behind neck, strict DB press, push press and jerk. (It has been my experience over the years that barbell presses of any kind with a very wide hand spacing may not be good for the shoulders of people with relatively long upper arms.

The same is true for pulldowns or chins behind the neck. Lanky frames, including mine, seem to add strength and mass better with medium- and close-spaced grips.)

4. **High pulls from floor**, power cleans from floor, or either one from the hang position. Standing high pulls with the trap bar will develop deltoid and upper back mass, and I love the feel of it.

5. **Bent over rows**, palms-facing (curl grip) chins or pulldowns with 10- to 12-inch hand spacing, one-DB rows, bent-arm pullovers. A little practiced but great movement for a short bulk program is the straight-arm pulldown from an overhead pulley.

6. **Deadlifts**, stiff-leg DL, leg lifts or stiff-legs with trap bar, partials in rack.

7. **Barbell curl**, alternate DB curl begun in "hammer" position, reverse grip bar curl for fore-arms. I do not think much of E-Z curl or preacher apparatus for anyone but competition bodybuilders.

8. **Donkey calf raises**, one-DB raises, standing machine, seated machine.

9. **All waist work**, including regular sit-ups, hanging leg raises, ab crunches, leg raise crunches on incline, controlled twisting movements.

10. **Shrug variations**, such as Kelso or lat shrug, bench shrug or any of such movements I describe in the text.

Bodybuilders and others tell us that "pelvic tilt" crunches are superior to regular sit-ups because they take the interior (psoas) muscles connecting the legs and hips to the upper torso out of the movement and isolate the abs. True. But that is exactly why athletes and especially lifters should be doing some of the old style as well as the new. They need those connections for overall strength, and that includes the obliques. Remember, a tiny waist on a "muscle man" is often a weak waist. The current "ideal" is simply false, except for "show" bodybuilding.

A classic way to train is to take one movement from each of the above listings and do them 3 x 10, in a full-body routine three times a week. Better would be to do the lower body moves for higher reps of eight to 15 and the upper body moves six to ten. Perhaps millions have trained this way, myself when a teen, and made good gains despite two-hour

Full Body Split Training Routines

Kelso's Routine #1

First Day
Squat, bench, high pulls (or alternates). 3-5 sets each.
Curls, calves. 3 sets each.
18-20 sets total

Second Day
Overhead press, deadlift or stiff-leg DL, rows or chins. 3 - 5 sets each (2 sets of stiff-leg DL is enough).
Flat bench DB press, waist work. 3 sets each.
18-20 sets total

Third Day (optional)
Front squats or trap bar leg lifts, close-grip bench on incline or dips, Kelso shrugs and stiff-leg deadlifts. Add curls, calves, 2 sets each, and you again have 18-20 sets total. Additional waist work should be done at home on off-days.

workouts. This type of training is often too demanding for one workout and presupposes good recovery ability and youth.

   To increase intensity and get enough rest so you can really gain, split these movements into two or more *full body* routines, with squat, bench, and cleans or high pulls one day, and deadlifts, overhead pressing, and rows or chins the other, using three to five sets of each exercise, with a two days of rest between workouts. One or two sets each of curls, calves and waist can be tacked on at the end. In this way, all body parts would be worked at least three times in two weeks. Splitting the work into upper body and lower body days, each done twice a week, is usually too much work for non-advanced trainees and for much older folk, unless on some kind of chemical support.

   How about this example of a split? I have done this type of routine about six months a year for the last four years, and it is very similar to the routine I wrote for Dell. His included more deep-breathing work, specifically by going to high-rep squats every other squat day.

Kelso's Routine #1

   First Day—Squat, bench, high pulls (or alternates): three to five sets each. Curls, calves: three sets each.

   Second Day—Overhead press, deadlift or stiff-leg DL, rows or chins: three to five sets each (two sets of stiff-leg DL is enough).

   Flat bench DB press, waist work: three sets each.

   18-20 sets total either *day*.

   An optional third day includes front squats or trap bar leg lifts, close grip bench on incline or dips, Kelso shrugs and stiff-leg deadlifts. Add two sets each of curl and calf and you again have 18-20 sets. Additional waist work should be done at home on off-days.

   Note: This would be a good place to use a five-set scheme on the major movements. Begin with a warm-up of eight to ten reps with 60% of single-rep maximum, another with about 70%, and then 3 x 5 with 80- 85%, using a constant weight.

   Here's another program I have used:

Kelso's Routine #2:

   First Day—Squat, incline press, rows or pulldowns, upright rows or standing presses.

   Second Day—Leg press AND deadlifts, each for 2 x 12-15, flat bench press, bar or DB's, lat shrugs, heavy curls.

   Both Days—Calves and waist work, each 2 x reps. Use the 4 x 8-12 basic scheme or the 5-set, your choice.

Full Body Split Training (continued)

Kelso's Routine #2

First Day
Squat, incline press, rows or pulldowns, upright rows or standing presses.

Second Day
Leg press AND deadlifts, each for 2 x 12-15, flat bench press, bar or DB's, lat shrugs, heavy curls.

Both Days
Calves and waist work, each 2 x reps.
Use the 4 x 8-12 basic scheme or the 5-set.

And another, using three of the best currently neglected movements: front squat, parallel bar dips and bent-arm pullovers, plus stiff-leg deadlifts. Think you wouldn't grow on that?

Train no more than three days in a week with full body routines. I personally find that as the weights get heavier over several months during a cycle, I must cut back to five workouts in two weeks and eventually to twice a week. Several times I have taken the heavy end of a general training cycle through three or four more weeks by dropping to three workouts in two weeks.

Folks infected by years of common bodybuilding "wisdom" will yell that such a program is not enough work. Or they'll complain that there's not anything in it for their rear delts or intercostals. One of "Kelso's Laws" (see Chapter 13) is that it is senseless to go on a "finishing" type bodybuilding program designed to produce definition and separation before you have some muscles to define or separate! What the average trainee and genuine "hard gainers" often refuse to believe is that "less is more" in their case. Thousands of people in the last few decades have trained for years with nothing much to show for it until they finally adopt "old-fashioned" methods like those I just sketched out.

A true high-rep squat program, where one does a total of only five or six *sets* in a workout, is even harder to sell. This classic method that has been turning mice into monsters for about 60 years is so simple that most trainees never give it a chance. After some full body warm-ups, one selects a weight that should allow 12-15 reps in the squat. By using a moderate pace and two or three or more deep breaths between each rep, and with a little help from your friends as spotters, force out 20! This is immediately followed by 20 reps of pullovers or flyes on the bench with a light weight. One or two other exercises are added and that's all.

When you can do 20 reps in the breathing squat with your own bodyweight, you're on your way. With 150% of bodyweight, you will have moved up a couple weight classes. Double bodyweight for twenty, or perhaps 400 lbs., and you should be incredible. It may take years to get there, but it's that simple.

The pattern is obvious. Squat, push, pull. Go home. Train twice a week maximum or when your body tells you you're ready to go again. Some prefer squat sets of 2 x 15. Reports are increasing of similar big gains with high rep deadlifts in the same workout pattern. The squat-style clean and jerk will work as the central exercise in a routine of this type by beginning with a weight that can be cleaned and pressed for eight reps. Continue the set with push presses and as that becomes too heavy, begin jerking. A full front squat should be done every rep.

Rotation of Routines

Two separate routines training three times a week: A-B-A, the first week, and B-A-B the second.

Twice a week: Monday and Thursday, or Tuesday and Friday, etc.

Five times in two weeks: Monday, Thursday, Saturday or Sunday, Tuesday or Wednesday, and Friday.

The secret of high-rep squats is to work hard, breathe hard and add weight a little at a time. Many old-timers used a cambered squat bar for comfort and balance; these bars have been around since the '30s and are now making a comeback. I recommend a four-month trial with these programs initially and then periodically throughout your training career. More information on these methods can be found in Strossen's *SUPER SQUATS*, in *Hardgainer* magazine, my own *The Kelso Shrug System* and in the writings of Peary Rader, Mark Berry, Bob Hoffman and others.

Thirty-five to 40 years ago you could read in *Iron Man* or *Strength & Health* that these types of training succeeded by lowering the metabolic rate and thus encouraging weight gains. I don't know of anyone defending that idea currently, but it does fit recent evidence that hormone release occurs in the first twenty minutes of training and continues for another twenty or thirty before tailing off. Plus, only big, multi-joint exercises will trigger that release.

I am in my mid-fifties while writing these words. I have trained with short, full-body workouts and with the type of split described above, taking at least two days rest between sessions for the last four years. (Older trainees may need more recovery time—some Masters powerlifters break for as much as ten days between intense, heavy squat or deadlift days.) My strength has gone up or recovered markedly. I'll never be what I was long ago, but this is fun! I am gaining muscular bodyweight at an age when most guys are looking for a place to nap. Some refuse to believe I'm not "on the juice." When I show them my simple routine, they don't believe THAT!

High-Rep Squat Training

Example routines:
1. **Behind neck press.** 3 x 12.
2. **Squat.** 1 x 20.
3. **Pullovers.** 1 x 20 (Joe Hise program)

1. **Squat.** 1 x 20.
2. **Pullovers.** 1 x 20.
3. **Bench press.** 3 x 10.
4. **Bent over row.** 3 x 10

1. **Squat.** 1 x 20.
2. **Pullovers.** 1 x 20.
3. **High pull from hang.** 3 x 6.
4. **Dips.** 3 x 8.

1. **Squat.** 1 x 20.
2. **Pullovers.** 1 x 20.
3. **Close grip bench.** 3 x 8.
4. **Kelso lat shrug.** 2 x 8-10

If you're tough: Add one set of 12 reps with the stiff-leg deadlift after the pullovers unless doing high pulls the same day.

High-intensity training, as advocated by Dr. Ken Leistner, Dick Connors, the H.I.T. Newsletter and others is another growing trend. Rather than the usual heavy weights and low reps, or lighter weights and high reps arrangements, this style calls for the highest weight and number of reps possible for a very limited number of sets. A few exercises are chosen for any one workout, and after a warm-up, are taken to the absolute limit. Many do only one, all-out set of each exercise. The Kelso's Routines above would do as a H.I.T. workout if done with fewer, extended sets.

Rep goals are set and weights adjusted so that many exercises—not just the squat—may be performed 15, 20, or even 30 reps on occasion. Many are working up to 20-30 reps in this manner with weights most people cannot do once! You can make great gains from this training style, but it's tough and requires extra recovery time, some spacing workouts four to eight days or more apart.

The folklore of this training tells of lots of locker room barfing and walking funny for days afterward. I've done cycles of twenty-rep squats and bench presses and even clean and jerks in the past, and recommend them to everyone. But I don't think a year-round, steady diet of this type of training is any wiser than maxing out on single lifts once a week. Nor would I recommend this style for everybody, certainly not for raw beginners and probably not for most older trainees unless they are experienced and in good shape. It is good to go all out fairly often, but not every workout, in my opinion. Just the commitments of everyday life may dictate that you can't. A longtime practice in training is to extend yourself on one to two movements during a workout and do the rest of your exercises more or less normally. The next workout, select different exercises for this treatment.

I have not filled this book with a lot of cheerleading and slogans like "no pain, no gain," urging the trainee to do or die. It is so obvious to me that a person has to do some work to succeed that I overlooked this aspect. But it is true, people. If you're not going to strive for progression in your training, you might as well stay home.

By the way, what Leistner and company refer to as H.I.T. appears to differ from methods of the same name seen in some bodybuilding mags. The latter emphasize very short rest periods between multiple sets of every exercise, taking the sets to failure. That is for bodybuilding contest preparation in my view, and not for general training.

To be fair, H.I.T. is relatively new and may be the wave of the future. Stranger things have happened in this game. At the opposite end of the spectrum are the "single lift" advocates who do extended, vigorous aerobic exercises for twenty or thirty minutes and then three singles in the 80-95% range of only two to four movements chosen for that day.

There are hundreds of known programs and rep/set schemes that can be attempted after basic training and everybody in the game has his or her favorites. Remember, there is no *one* correct way to train. A really subversive secret of weight training is that almost any balanced program will work pretty well as long as you're eating right and don't overtrain. It depends on what you are training for.

After a few months on the type of split I suggested above, you can start adding close grip presses and shrugs, dips and stiff-leg deadlifts in place of some of those I listed above. I absolutely do not recommend maximum single attempts more than every three months. After six months or so, I do recommend what I call bench shrugs and Kelso shrugs worked in when appropriate (see Chapters 2 and 4).

If no drugs, what? I am not going to get into a long discussion here about the pros and cons of bodybuilding drug use. I'll address that subject later on. The first thing is to make sure of proper eating habits and basic nutrition. It is far cheaper and more beneficial to eat correctly from the start than to spend a fortune on supplements. If you are not going to eat properly, you might as well not train. Learn to cook if there's nobody in your kitchen who can be relied on. Can you boil water? If so, you're half way home.

Back in the fifties we all loaded up on raw milk and peanut butter and soy-based protein powder. We got bigger and stronger. Got gas, too. The bodybuilders discovered they also stayed smooth. Soy protein products are usually an inferior source, and one study cited in the "H.I.T. Newsletter" showed that excessive amounts of soy protein reduces testosterone production in males. The problem with most highly-touted supplements is that they are too expensive for what they deliver. Three-fourths of them seem to fade away after a few years because they don't work, or don't work well enough to justify the expense. In my opinion and experience, beef-liver tabs were a good source of protein and energy 40 years ago, and they still are. Both a vitamin-mineral tab and an egg and milk protein powder are safe bets.

Just about anything ending in "ol" will not do anything significant, although there is great current interest in new plant, horn and hoof derivatives from Asia and the old Soviet Union. Warning: many of these exotic Asian herbs, powders and insect fungus compounds you've been hearing about contain banned substances. Many supplements available in stores and by mail, some with oriental-sounding names, contain that and other ingredients, often not listed in the ads, that are on the banned list of the IOC, the IAAF and the IPF. It might not be illegal for the companies to include such fairy dust often without warning the buyer, but it is sure irresponsible.

Powdered "shotgun" compounds that have a little of everything seem to help some when taken before and after workouts. So does eating pasta or rice and fruit.

Many drug-free trainees who want strength and size mainline food instead. They eat five to six times a day—some carbs and a little protein about 45 minutes before workouts and again immediately after. Then a big protein load within an hour. Please, study up on this subject, but spend your money on food first.

I sketched out a program for Dell and told him to keep in touch. "But what'll I do with all those pills I bought?"

"Take 'em out in the lake and throw 'em in your lunker hole."

Two years later he had gained sixteen pounds. He also caught an 11-lb. 9-oz. bucket-mouth bass out of his secret fishing spot.

Could it be? Naah . . .

Speaking of food, let me illustrate just how earth-shaking the advice I send my correspondents can be.

The last letter in the stack Coach Koltuniak brought me was from Calcutta: India, not Texas. I had heard from the fellow several times over the years. He lived in a poor fishing village on the coast. His first letter back in '79 said he couldn't gain weight as the whole village sold their fish catch to buy "muhi," a poi-like carbohydrate paste which made up almost their entire diet.

I suggested he save back and eat a fish a day and explained about protein needs. He tried it a while and was beefing up until his father caught him and beat him.

I wrote a letter to his dad and included a picture of Steve Reeves in some kind of a Sinbad outfit and told him that all the sons of the village could look like Steve if they ate a fish a day. Pretty soon the entire village was into it and getting healthier. Then I got a letter from a U.S. government agency telling me that I had created an international incident by interfering in the internal affairs of a foreign nation, and my scheme was playing havoc with the local economy and disrupting traditional values.

My bodybuilding fisherman explained that the village headman was bought off by the muhi dealers. After a couple of food riots, the young man and his dad proceeded to become what passes for wealthy in the village by bootlegging fish. Shows you what kind of clout I have.

When Miss Stotts heard this story, she decided I was O.K. after all.

CHAPTER 7

Boxes, Belts and Beer Mines

I was driving through the state forest down in southeast Texas, keeping one eye out for ivory-billed woodpeckers and the other for Lope Delk and his portable sawmill. Yes, I know they're supposed to be extinct—the woodpeckers, that is—although Lope's peculiar breed is getting a little rare as well. There's still a lot of wildlife to be seen on the back trails, including the armadillo in his natural habitat: dead by the side of the road.

I wanted to drop off a copy of a squat routine for Lope that I had just picked up in Hemphill. I saw the smoke from the old donkey engine through a gap in the trees and turned in down a logging road. What I saw before me is indelibly stamped in my memory. Lope and the weight club hardhead were rolling around on the ground like a pair of dervishes in the last stages of religious ecstasy. They were laughing so hard that they were incoherent (which wasn't so hard for them) and near to passing out.

Preacher Harley was jammed butt-first in a number-two washtub full of iced-down beer, with about ten feet of six-inch donkey engine belt wrapped around him. The belt had snapped during a log drag and one end of it ricocheted around and slapped the Preacher across the seat of his ample pants, lifted him five feet up in the air and dropped him tail first into the tub. He was groaning and going on about having been "smitten hip and thigh," while alternately holding his rear with both hands and trying to get out of the freezing tub.

Squatlo had one end of the belt in his mouth and was trying to kill it. That was the end wrapped around Preacher's neck. Every time Preacher lurched up, the mutt hauled him back down. Kind of hard to operate at cross-purposes with an enraged sixty-pound, chicken-lovin' duck dog.

When the snorting and choking and moaning finally died down and the Preacher was back on his feet (where he stayed for a week or two), Lope opened another before he realized I was standing there. He took a deep breath, crammed his old leather hat down over one eye and started working the sand, leaves and beer out of his Wyatt Earp mustache.

"Kelso, I ain't had so much fun since the night we robbed the beer mine."

Now, despite rumors around town and at the bar at the Scoot 'N Boot, I was not, I say again, *not* in on that.

Long before I even moved to East Texas, a brewery train derailed out in the woods and dumped sixteen boxcars worth of cases of bottled beer into the blackberry bushes. Word got around and the authorities had to use axe handles and shot guns to stop the souvenir hunting. They brought in backhoes and bulldozers and buried the beer along the right-of-way. Posted armed guards to prevent looting until they could get the wreck cleared and bring in another train to haul the beer out.

The brewery and the railroad eventually gave up on reclaiming the beer. The area is swampy in parts and great stacks of cased beer are said to lie waiting, twenty feet down. Midnight prospecting went on for years, and great schemes for recovering the treasure of the "The Lost Beer Mine" are still being hatched in bars and cafes.

The rumor around is that Lope and some of his "cousins" (the nickname "Cuz" means "unindicted co-conspirator" in those parts) showed up a night or two later with their own backhoe and trucks and bribed or threatened the guards. Got out with 483 cases of longnecks.

Lope got busy and converted his Uncle Whale's barbecue joint out on the old Kilgore highway into a honky-tonk and had a license in about two weeks 'cause another uncle was in the legislature. That's Texas politics, and how the Scoot 'N Boot came to be.

Uncle Whale is about 5'7" tall and maybe 135 lbs. after Sunday dinner but is, uh, legendarily, er, blessed: thus his name. Say one word about it and he'd try to whale the daylights out of you. But I digress.

Maybe a week after the Preacher's gluteal baptism, we all got together for a workout and to try out the "new" squat routine. It turned out to be a variation on pyramiding. Nothing special. Then one of the boys who had been on the Athens High state champion powerlifting team showed us a good idea for finding squat depth.

He took a rubber tarp tie-down, or bungee cord, and hooked the ends to the uprights on the power rack so that the cord stretched across from one to the other. He positioned it down low so that when he broke parallel in the squat, his rear hit the cord. Then the kid sank the squat another half inch for good measure and recovered. The idea is to train to that cord long enough so the lifter will know where he is at meet time. The Wampus Cat Club used that trick from then on with good results.

Lope watched all this with great concentration. He had his "Southern engineer" look on his face.

Next workout Lope was back with some clamps and hooks and about four feet of the belt we'd unwrapped from around Preacher Harley's neck after we got him out of the washtub. Lope rigged the belt across the power rack at the height he'd need to hit parallel. Then he loaded the bar with about 300 lbs. and lowered into a squat with it. Sat on the belt. It sagged maybe an inch. When Lope started up the belt gave him a little sling-shot boost. I don't have to tell you how strong a donkey engine belt is, do I? Take it on faith.

We all got on the program: squatting to the belt, sinking into it and recovering. We varied the belt height so that some squats were higher than parallel and some lower. Preacher Harley eased his ample glutes down to the belt and gingerly put the full weight of the bar and himself on it. He looked heavenward and crowed, "Vengeance is mine!"

Lope and the hardhead went to Coach Koltuniak and tried to get him to help them manufacture and sell the belts, but after the fiasco with the bench press benches made from nine-inch oil field pipe, Coach Bubba was out of town permanently whenever they had a "bidness" brainstorm.

Couple of odd things about Lope: he adopted the hardhead as a sort of reclamation project; maybe the boy reminded Lope of himself at an early age, I don't know. Lope was also always inventing something or starting a new project. A lot of his efforts were doomed at the gate; a lot succeeded, considering all the "bidnesses" he had the keys to.

Years before Lope built his first power rack for the school weight room, he was using overhead chains and planks and boxes of various heights and carpenter's saw horses and automobile jacks for stands and safety devices for partial lifts. As was I. As were generations of iron men before us.

Lope had several pairs of hooks with T-handles, like stevedores or packing house workers use to move crates and carcasses. They were different lengths, 12 to 24 inches long. They were and are fine for practicing partial deadlifts at different heights. We also experimented with adjustable-length cargo straps borrowed from a long-haul moving company. Rigged a hook on 'em. The great Paul Anderson is known to have done partial deadlifts of over 1000 pounds for reps *in this manner*.

A spin-off of the bungee cord-engine belt tests was to use them under the feet while doing chins in the power rack. The small boost one gets allows for a cheating technique so the trainee can get more reps in before his hands and arms give out.

Lope's squatting into a belt method is related to the box squat. I have never understood why this movement is neglected. It has gone in and out of favor several times in my training lifetime. A box or bench is positioned behind the lifter so that his seat touches it at the low point of the squat. One use is a touch-and-go from the box, set at a height for a legal squat. Like the bungee cord trick, this trains the lifter to know exactly how low he must go.

Another is to sink on to the box so that the muscles are partially relieved of the weight and then recover. The depth of the squat can be varied by raising and lowering the height of the box by using planks under it or on it. The pause at the bottom requires all the involved muscles to engage at the same time when the recovery is begun. The theory is the same as when using extended pauses at the chest for training the bench press.

Remember that round footstool or hassock that your grandfather had in front of his easy chair in the living room? Well, dig it out of the garage and use it to squat to. It is filled with tightly packed straw or wood shavings and will give when you sink into it. Sacks of feed can also be used.

Some criticize the box movement as being dangerous. They believe that the spine is compressed when the trainee sits to the bench with the bar on the shoulders. I absolutely agree—*if* the lifter tries to bounce off the bench or lowers himself too fast. The poundages used should be built up over time in a moderate progression which allows the body to adjust and strengthen. Using a hassock or any other yielding "box" or a belt would relieve that potential problem somewhat.

Even better might be to set the pins low in a power rack so that when you wiggle under the bar, you are in the deep squat position with thighs parallel to start with. After rising (you hope!) and sinking down again, let the rack relieve you of the weight briefly, then drive up another rep. Trap bars, hip belts and "magic circles" can also give you this dead-stop benefit. The same effect can be had in bench training by setting the bar in the power rack just above the chest on full inhale. These rack movements are known to many as the "bench start" and the "squat start." They are replacing older methods rapidly and are widely advocated.

When I was eighteen and weighed maybe 190 pounds at 6'1", I was stuck at 255 lbs. for five reps in the high-bar style squat. Roy Smith, who was maybe 65-70 at the time and a former world record holder in one-hand lifts, showed me the box technique at the old Dallas YMCA. I improved drastically, doing 285 x 5 after two weeks of box workouts. My bodyweight was up to 208 lbs. when I joined the Army a year later. Youth is a factor no one has yet packaged.

That was in 1955. Box squats are in the literature of the game back to the 1930s, at least. Rebound movements also go way back. Remember Joe Hise's "hopper" platform for deadlift training? Or those old-timers who placed stacks of boards on each side of their press bench and bounced enormous overloads off them? Bouncing weights is now out of fashion. Fred Howell is the great exponent of these methods. Not only is he the most prolific of Iron Game writers, but his articles on these subjects still appear regularly in training magazines. At this writing, he is still handling astonishingly heavy weights at an age when many men are in nursing homes.

The idea behind these odd devices or exercises is to find ways to continue the set, use greater weights, and get as many muscles to fire at the same time as possible during the transition point of the exercise or lift. Pausing at the chest for a long count during a bench press or at the bottom of a squat requires full muscle involvement. Working these techniques into programs will result in bigger totals.

E vidence of this is the success of Louie Simmons and the powerlifters from the West Side Barbell Club of Columbus, Ohio. A book could and should be written about the ideas and exploits of Simmons. Whatever is said, he is one of the most innovative of coaches and equipment developers.

His lifters rarely perform the actual competition lifts. Instead, they pursue box squats with and without lockout at the top, close-grip incline benches, partials, and pause training; deliberately do some exercises "wrong"; and usually work with only 60-80% of maximum for the lifts in order to increase speed. You guys who try to max once a week, please take note.

By the way, when the drive belt and washtub incident happened, more or less as I told it, the Club hardhead was still drinking and partying, and his strength was up and down like a yo-yo. Booze causes dehydration, screws up liver function and even causes temporary inflammation of muscle cells and membranes. Too much alcohol too often, and your strength and recovery ability start downhill.

I spent ten years on the road playing the guitar and living that lifestyle during the years when I should have been making my greatest gains in the weight room. I don't mean to sound like Preacher Harley (even he spikes his orange Nehi sometimes) but a serious lifter can't make gains prospecting for beer mines.

CHAPTER 8

L aVonda Sue, We Love You

I'm sitting around in my office out to the college when LaVonda Sue Braley comes in and announces she has a problem. Maybe I haven't told you enough about LaVonda—she of the Etruscan temple dancer's eyes that could call a grown man to tears at 200 yards.

She was not only my secretary, but one of the school cheerleaders. Nobody wore the school colors better then LaVonda. They and about six others matched her eyes. Anyway, her problem was this: she wanted to lift with the Club at the Regional Collegiates, but Coach Koltuniak wanted her doing back flips at the Pine Woods Invitational the same weekend.

So did the school Prez, the basketball team, her boyfriend, the blue-hair brigade up in the Admin. office, the student body and the dorm mothers. Now, with eight cheerleaders on the squad you would think that they could do without her for a couple of non-league games. The tournament, however, was for MONEY. It also got a lot of publicity that the Prez insisted was good for recruiting new students. Eight or nine thousand fans would shell out $2.50 each for the games and half of East Texas would see, hear and read about it through the media.

I don't have to tell you how many folks work themselves up into a frenzy over a handful of junior college powerlifters, do I?

Right.

LaVonda hadn't competed in powerlifting before. She ran track and played basketball and had gymnastic training. She knew all the cheerleader's tricks and stunts. I knew she'd be a fine lifter. But more important, she wanted to give it a shot. LaVonda worked out with the Club off and on, but there were so many demands on her time that she couldn't get to a contest with us. Social pressure in any small town or school can be enormous.

When LaVonda let it be known that she wanted to go to the meet, the administration and the Coach informed her that her "duty" was to the school. The blue-hairs in the office told her that no decent man would ever marry a girl who engaged in such an activity. The dorm mothers clucked that even if one did marry her, she wouldn't be able to bear children.

POWERLIFTING BASICS, TEXAS-STYLE

Her boyfriend told her it was O.K. if other guys' wives or girlfriends wanted to lift "to please their man," but no girlfriend of his was gonna' do such an unsuitable thing. (Why are so many men insecure on this issue?) When the young women in the Club heard about his remark, their response wasn't "suitable," either.

Just what was so special about LaVonda, anyway? We've all seen people who just flat have the magic, whether curse or blessing. If all the cheerleaders from both schools were out on the floor giving their best for the Wampus Cats and the Blue Devils or what have you, and LaVonda was standing by the scorer's table eating nachos, every handheld cam recorder in the field house would be trained on her! The consensus was that the tournament would go broke and the gym would slide downhill into the Neches if she didn't show up.

You may remember that LaVonda had the uncanny ability to cut right to the truth, often at my expense, and did not suffer fools. Like when Coach Koltuniak was dumb enough to hit on her. She figured he was "being ugly" by telling her she couldn't lift with us because she had put him down.

I, with my vaunted integrity, weaseled around and suggested that the basketball tourney was a prior commitment she should honor and that she could lift with us next time. She stared at my 1955 North Texas Open trophy for a minute, and then left.

As we pulled out from in front of the gym on the day before the Regionals, LaVonda and the cheerleaders stood by to bring us luck while a crowd of students already there for the first game of the Invitational gave us a send-off. The Prez and Coach Koltuniak smugly wished us well and thanked me for talking sense to LaVonda. I also saw Lope Delk and Preacher Harley in the crowd grinning like 'possums. I didn't think much of it as they rarely missed a home game.

Next morning in Austin, I'm lining up the gang for the weigh-in when in walks Lope and the Preacher—still grinning—and LaVonda. She said she'd kinda' like to lift if I didn't mind. They had jumped into Lope's country customized van and driven half the night with LaVonda asleep in the back. This was after the Wampus Cats had put the Falfurrias Skeeters away by 17, with LaVonda stirring up the fans.

Lope noticed that I was a little slack-jawed at the turn of events, not to mention that I was wondering where I'd get another teaching job. He explained that they had gotten her entry blanks in six weeks ago and liked driving at night anyway.

Oh.

Naturally, her showing up was a big boost to the rest of the Club. LaVonda lifted like a veteran and made eight of nine attempts, pulling into third place with her last deadlift. The other kids took four or five place and show trophies. Yeah, I play the horses sometimes.

I didn't have an entry over 181 that day, so we were through by 3:30. I was shooting the breeze with Terry Todd and putting out job feelers with some old friends, when Lope comes over and allows that if I'm not too busy, the tournament finals started at 7:45 and we might think about hitting the road and saving our collective rear ends by getting LaVonda to the game on time.

What he actually said was,

"Kelso, we don't get her back, it'll strap a harelip on everybody in the county."

I told Lope and the Preacher that there wasn't any way to get back in four hours. More 'possum grins.

We loaded and lit out over every nonmapped two-lane and back road, paved or not, that Lope had ever traveled or heard of, me gunning that old school bus to keep the van in sight.

We skidded up to the front door of the gym at 7:42 to find a dozen police cars, reporters, the Prez and half the town milling around in a panic. The whole county thought LaVonda kidnapped, or worse, gone with us, when she didn't show for the pep rally. The Prez started screaming at me about responsibility and teaching jobs in the Yukon in the same breath.

The muttering crowd surged closer.

It was getting ugly.

Then the school bus door opened and out pranced LaVonda in her cheerleader outfit with the rest of the lifters right behind her in their squat suits and Club T-shirts waving their trophies over their heads. They formed a line and strutted like a rap group into the gym. The crowd exploded like we'd just won the NCAA, and the band struck up Wabash Cannonball. The basketball team had been moping around and throwing up air balls during warm-ups but broke into grins and raced over and carried LaVonda around the gym on their shoulders.

The Prez, that soul of constancy, was still lecturing me when Lope and the Preacher lifted him by the elbows and carried him over to the scorer's table to pose for pictures with the lifters, LaVonda, the Booster Club and the roundballers for the Tyler papers. The constant Prez immediately produced a glowing imitation of an enlightened educator surrounded by adoring students and fans. He ain't so dumb.

This mess sorted out like a storybook ending. The ball team won the game, I kept my job and LaVonda dumped the boy friend. The Prez later gave credit for the huge success of the weekend to the administration's desire that every student achieve his or her dreams. I tried to thank LaVonda for bailing me out. She quietly cast her aroused lemur's eyes on me.

LaVonda Sue Special

This routine is not something I would recommend widely. However, the young lady who did it prospered on it. She did it for two months, pre-contest, which seems about right to me. Train twice a week.

1. **Power-style squat.** Warm-ups, 3 x 4-6.
2. **Bench press.** Warm-ups, 3 x 4-6.
3. **Deadlift.** Warm-ups, 3 x 4-6.

That's it. Why she didn't overtax her lower back, I'll never know. My guess, that's right, guess, is that she did not ever extend herself to the point of failure. She was training alone, which is risky business unless using safety stands or working in a properly set power rack, especially for the squat and bench press. I would convert this routine into a basic "heavy and light" (see Chapter 13).

"I didn't do it for them, Mr. Kelso, and not for you. I did it for me."

She had made up her mind to do both the B-ball tournament and the PL contest right after that meeting with me. She sneaked into the weight room after hours a couple nights a week for two months before the meet. Trained by the light of the moon to keep her secret. LaVonda used short intense workouts of only three sets of four to six reps for each of the three lifts. The cheerleading and other sports she played gave her an aerobic base and conditioning.

I suppose the reader might be wondering by now what the point of this story is. I don't recommend her training program but it worked for her. Wherever LaVonda is these days, my money is on her being in control of her own life. She never wanted to be a strength star or even state champ; she wanted to lift with us at that meet on that day and she did.

Most of us don't have her kind of magic, but pure, no-excuses, no-obstacles-allowed determination can make magic happen.

CHAPTER 9

You Can't Shrug It Off

It was the kind of gym I like: older part of town, a deli next door and a laundromat across the street. Rooms to rent upstairs and a bus stop out front. Not a potted plant to be seen, no hanging ferns, no lavender carpets, child care pens or sprout sandwiches. No electronic gizmos from Bulgaria to measure the molecular viscosity of toe nails.

It was a black iron gym, before chrome, dating back to a time when meets were held on the basketball floor of the YMCA and lifters often hung around to enter the bodybuilding contest.

Wood. Iron. Leather. Lifting platforms. The place had that feel and smell of authenticity. There were posters on the wall touting boxing matches of long ago, old York and Jowett training charts, 8 x 10's that used to be glossy, autographed by Clancy Ross, Jack Dellinger and Argentina Rocca. Sacramento has its memories: Bill Pearl had his first gym there, and Chester O. Teegarden and the young Tommy Kono trained at the now-vanished downtown Y, back in the early fifties.

The main thing at this place was the gang that trained there. Older crowd, ex-competitors, has-beens, never-wases, guys doing their favorite movements. No small part of it was just hanging around and getting out of the house. The owner was burned out and had long since quit watching the floor and coaching the members. He spent his days next door at the deli having coffee.

It was early summer and the redheaded 148-pounder was finishing her B.A. back in Texas. We had partnered-up toward the end of my tenure at Pine Woods, and I had come out West in advance to find a house before she started graduate school in late August. I was spending a hot Sacramento June working on some articles and doing a little light training. I was kinda' burned out myself and swore I wouldn't get involved with any more clubs or coaching.

But I did.

There were three college-age boys at the gym who had decided to get into their first power meet. Rich Peters was bringing his traveling circus around in the spring. No more driving hundreds of miles to contests; just wait, Rich would bring one by, hauling everything needed in a big ole truck, hurtling through the Great American hinterland (Topeka on Friday, boys!), and if there's an off night, well, set up on the edge of town and start something.

Peters' NASA (Natural Athlete Strength Association) has become a formidable and popular operation, with classes for the ex-user, the pure, the never-touch-the stuff, the three-years clean, the natural and the repentant. My impression is that it's a good gang to get started with because there're so many slots for those on the way up. A lifter might enter the novice, open and pure flights in the same meet when it's allowed. Is it true that one meet had 120 lifters and passed out 168 trophies?

The boys were arguing about how to set up a program. The heaviest built guy was lording it over the others. He knew that the best way to train was the way he trained. He was the strongest, wasn't he? There wasn't any need to do all those fancy routines and figure percentages, he opined. All a guy needed was to do the basics; if a person had what it takes, he'd succeed.

Now, there is much truth in that. The problem is, that attitude will win a lot of local meets, but won't do much good at state or national contests because everybody there has got what it takes. All other things being equal, the guy who uses his brain to set up his training is going to win most often in the long run. Then he said,

"With my squat and bench I oughta' win easy."

There I sat in my Wampus Cat Club t-shirt. I couldn't take it. "What about the deadlift?" I asked.

The local hero shrugged it off.

"I just let my squat take care of it and do a few rows. All you need is to do them twice a month or so. Nothing to the deadlift, anyway."

Translation: "I don't like deadlifts, have made no progress in a year; I can smoke the squat and bench pretty good, but my ego prevents me from facing up to the facts."

I introduced myself and allowed that I had actually been to a couple of meets. Offered to help. Knew the rules. The boys bought in. Said they'd read some of my articles and such.

Every time I get in one of these situations I feel a little like the crusty but benign gym owner in the old "Keys to Progress" series by John McCallum. Veterans will remember the stories about the long-suffering coach and his charges that appeared in *Strength & Health* back in the sixties. John generally called for basic workouts, primarily for the full body and without a lot of nonsensical frills. He used a cast of continuing characters to carry the stories and to present new plots. It's an old device, sort of like a sit-com, and was not unknown to Chaucer and the ancient Greeks.

McCallum is no longer with us, but his humor and surpassing talent left a writing legacy that dozens of Iron Game writers have been influenced by, myself included. Too many try to copy his style but have neither his skills, originality nor ability to bring characters to life and sustain a series.

But the lads at the gym in Sacramento were not the knuckleheads usually found in those types of stories. They were average guys with varying training knowledge and experience. Plus the usual amount of misinformation and a tendency to peacock around the gym.

They all used the sumo-style deadlift. Furthermore, they practiced sumo fashion every deadlift workout. I told 'em that Lamar Gant, Sylvester Anderson, Ausby Alexander, world champs all, and dozens of other record holders used conventional style. The choice depends on body type and arm length, not the style itself. Secondly, *doing* sumo-style is not the best way to *train* for sumo-style.

The first deadlift session I had the gang max out and I wrote down the results. Said not a word. I went over to the lifting platform and commenced doing high pulls from the floor, clean grip. I set up like an Olympic lifter and pulled the bar up to the breastbone. Lots of leg drive, chin and elbows high, full body extension. The next set I added weight and pulled to the belt.

The gang trailed along as I went over to the incline bench and got on it face down. The boys handed the bar off the floor and I started shrugging up toward the chest, crunching my scapula together and a little down toward the tailbone. Not up toward the ears. Kept my arms straight and got a full stretch between reps.

The gym owner watched from his office. When the bar was back on the floor, he grunted and went out on the street.

"O.K., give me five sets of five on the high pulls and four sets of eight on the shrug," I said.

The big boy was confused.

"Shrug? That don't look like any shrug I ever saw."

Then one of the others came up with a line I've been saving for years.

"Man, you think a shrug is an Italian mannerism."

I loved it. I went on.

"Increase the weight on the pulls every set and decrease on the shrugs. Use straps if you need 'em, but your grip will improve if you don't. Do these instead of your deadlift workout for a couple months."

"But Coach, when do we deadlift?"

"September . . ."

Six weeks later I walked in carrying a device about five feet long with plate sleeves on each end and two interior bars bent to make a diamond shape. The Gerard Trap Bar. The gang stared. Somebody in the back muttered that he'd seen one before and it weren't no good because you can't bench with it. Right.

I stood in the middle of the bar and started doing a squat deadlift move with it, stopping and setting up at the bottom of each rep. I also showed them the shrug and high pull with the trap bar. Then I took 'em over to the power rack and put a straight bar in it, with the pins set about two inches below where the bar would be at the completion of a deadlift. Piled on maybe 85% of my max deadlift. Took a clean grip and a conventional stance and just straightened up like finishing a deadlift and pulled my shoulders back. Big deal.

"Coach, how come you're not using a competition grip, and ain't your hands too wide?"

"Because I want you to develop your grip, and the bar isn't heavy enough at this stage to pull out of your hands. You shouldn't have any trouble with that till you get way over what you can max now. This is a short range move. Change your grip when you start droppin' the bar. Straps later, maybe. The grip's wide because I want to make the movement a little tougher. This is for strength building, not performance.

"I want 4 x 8 with the Trap Bar and 5 x 5 on the power rack. Use as much weight as you can at the top setting. When the reps get easy, lower the pins a notch. When you get to the bottom in a month or so, go back to the original setting and add some weight. When you've finished the rack pulls, go do 3 x 8 with one-hand DB rows. You do these on the same day as the Trap Bar lifts, which are going to build your hip and leg drive."

I told them to squat and bench the other workout day, using high bar squats some days and very wide foot stance squats another. I hauled in a cambered bar from the weight barn behind Teegarden's house near the northside Air Force base for these.

"These 'wide foots' will help your squat *and* your sumo deadlift. Plus, do a few sets of wide foot placement leg presses both days. Keep your feet on the upper half of the press plate. No regular benches at all for a couple months. Instead try close grip benches, thumbs touching the outer pecs, on the incline. Then some flat bench DB presses and finish with one or two sets of bench shrugs. In the fall we'll work in reverse grip benches for a cycle."

"But, Coach, what about triceps work?"

"That's what I just said."

As the months went by, I got to know the young men pretty well and often shared post-workout chow downs and bull sessions. One day we went next door to the deli and tried some of the yuppified Cajun cooking. The big boy eventually located a shrimp in his gumbo. "Coach, how come everybody's stronger now than in the old days? Is it all drugs?"

I thought about it. It sure isn't *nouvelle cuisine*. Here's more or less how I replied.

I'm not sure everybody is. For one thing, there is a helluva lot higher percentage of the population training now. The number of people in the heavier classes is expanding. Growth in the size of the population and leisure time are related. Diets and training info are better, and sports medicine and nutrition are becoming a science. Performances in all sports have improved. Drugs and isolated compounds are a factor. But strangely enough, many drug free records often rival or exceed those of known drug users.

Today's equipment is superior, although any old-timer knows you can become hellacious with nothing but a barbell and a level surface to put it on. Many old timers' records are still on the books. They didn't have the support gear that lifters now use, the "nutritional" aids or the leisure that so many now seem to have. Don Reinhoudt and Jon Cole squatted over 900 more than two decades ago while wearing wrestling singlets and thin training belts. (Cole also benched 610 and made a 430 clean and jerk in that era.) The competitive lifts have changed. Few indeed are now trying to one-hand bent press 275 pounds, back lift 4000, or rock a standing bar of 500 lbs. on to the shoulders for squats. On the other hand, the bench press is a new lift, historically.

There is a psychological factor as well. I've got a harebrained theory that there were "four-minute mile" barriers in weight training. Remember that when the mark was finally passed, all kind of runners did it as well very shortly afterwards? When Hideki Inaba of Japan made the first four times bodyweight lift in competition over twenty years ago, it astonished everybody. Now such lifts are more or less commonplace. Lamar Gant and a very few others have made *five* times bodyweight lifts in powerlifting.

The theory could be applied to Steve Stanko's breaking of the "unattainable" 1000 lbs. total in weightlifting and Pat Casey being way ahead of his time in the bench press. Maybe the passing of 1000 in the squat and 700 in the bench by a handful of current guys is raising the level for all.

There are men now lifting who have Paul Anderson's 1200-lb. squat in the back of their minds. What women have accomplished and are reaching for is even more mind-boggling. When the impossible is reached, the possible becomes attainable. That's not a bad saying, is it?

O ne thing more. When I was a kid struggling in the Dallas YMCA with old York sets, watching Sid Henry working toward the national weightlifting title, I'd slap on four wide-rimmed 45-lb. plates with the big flanges (225 lbs.) and tell myself "that thing ain't as heavy as it looks." But it did *look* as heavy when viewed from the front as a bar loaded with four 50-kilo plates does today.

Putting on a pair of fives may be "nothin'" to some, but there's a lot of difference between 10 lbs. and 10 kilos. The conversion to kilogram sets is a factor. Putting on a pair of fives now has become what it was long ago. Also, I believe that the advent of the streamlined Olympic barbell plate had a terrific impact on the psychologies of lifters everywhere. Plus, with the thinner plates, the balance of the bar was moved in toward the lifter to his advantage. These factors may have had as much to do with the skyrocketing poundages in recent decades as the

Pre-Competition Cycles

First Cycle
Three workouts a week. Alternate workouts. All sets and reps listed are suggestions, not holy writ.

A Day
1. **High bar squat.** 3-4 x 10-15.
2. **Leg press.** 2 x 15-20.
3. **Close grip incline BP.** 3 x 8-10.
4. **Flat bench DB press.** 3 x 8-10.
5. **Bench shrug.** 1-2 x 8.

B Day
1. **High pull off floor.** 4 x 5.
2. **Kelso shrug/incline.** 3 x 8.
3. **Pulldowns/chins.** 3 x 8-10.
4. **Stiff-leg DL.** 1-2 x 10-12.
5. **Tinkering: curls, calves.**

Fifth week: Go for triples in the competition lifts. Take a break.
Tenth week: Max out lifts. Take a break.

If you are a sumo-style deadlifter, you may want to use that style for a few warm-up sets throughout the first two cycles.

proliferation of anabolic steroids at the same time. Am I nuts?

Well, yeah, could be.

With ten months to prepare, I set the gang up with three cycles of roughly three months each, allowing for holidays and school exam periods. We'd skip a workout or two if there was any sign of overtraining.

Remember, this is for people who have been training for some time, for a first-time competition well in the future. There is nothing mysterious about cycling. Cycles are begun with higher reps and moderate weights for three or four weeks, a middle period of six to eight weeks with a higher number of sets and lowered reps, and then three to four weeks with sets of two to five reps leading to a max-out day or contest. You then take a short layoff and resume by beginning the program over but adjusting all starting weights to approximately 5-10% higher than those used to begin the previous cycle. Older trainees may find shorter cycles and more frequent layoffs more effective.

If you have no Trap Bar available, a hip belt or "magic circle" or similar apparatus may be used. If these are not available, or you don't want to bother, then add more stiff-leg DL's, and do your leg presses on B Day with several foot positions and/or wide stance squats.

Many will yell at this point that this too strenuous a program for a ten-week cycle. Hold on a second. If that's what you think, begin the second and third cycles with one or even two weeks of working back up with higher rep sets—and—take an extra day or two between workouts whenever you feel that you are not fully recovered from the last one. There is no rigid days-per-week schedule during the last cycle. I don't believe in excessively organized schedules based on complicated steps. Why? Simply because everyone *is* different, and most people leading normal lives have trouble sticking to them.

Everybody, please quit trying to set up the perfect training schedule based on a rigid order of so

Pre-Competition Cycles *(continued)*

Second cycle
Two days a week. First five weeks:

A Day
1. **Bench press.** 5 x 5, or 6 x 4.
2. **Reverse grip, or close grip bench press.** 2 x 8.
3. **Squat.** 5 x 5, or 6 x 4 (squat starts in rack).
4. **Leg press.** 2 x 15-20.

B Day
1. **Trap Bar leg lifts.** 4 x 8.
2. **Partial pulls in rack.** 5 x 5.
3. **One-DB row.** 3 x 8.
4. **Tinkering: curls, calves.**

Fifth week: Go for triples in the lifts. Take a break.

Second five weeks: first week, high reps, moderate weights. Then:

A Day
1. **Squat.** Same.
2. **Squat starts or box squats.** Same.
3. **"Touch 'n go" BP warm-ups.** 2 x 8.
4. **Bench starts in rack.** 3 x 5; lock-outs or pin pushes: 3 x 3.

many workouts or increases a week for this or that lift or body part. For most people, bench or bench assistance workouts can be performed slightly more often than squat sessions, and direct deadlifting less than either. (That last may be a myth of powerlifting; Olympic weightlifters often work the lower back two to three times a week.)

It is your ability to recover that dictates how often you train. Teens can bounce back faster than thirty-year-olds. No two trainees are alike. A big recent trend is to train three days a week: squats—Monday, bench—Wednesday and deadlift—Friday. Some would add a light bench day on Saturday, and some light leg work to the Friday session. Others, usually older, are squatting heavy as little as every ten days, with some leg presses, Trap Bar work or high bar squats on DL day. But none of this is carved in stone.

"This shit is getting too complicated."

That is a direct quote from two-time world champion Ausby Alexander during a discussion of training methods in my apartment in Tochigi following his guest appearance at the Japan Men's National in 1991. Ausby is gentle spoken for a Marine Gunnery Sergeant, but his frustration with conflicting and complicated training theories is understandable. I'm with Ausby.

The powerlifting routine used by more people over the years than any other is a twice-a-week program calling for heavy squats and bench and maybe some rows one day, deadlift or DL assistance, light chest and light leg the other. "Light" means moderate weight on the lifts or assistance work, that is, eight to twelve reps. "Heavy" is roughly four to six. It shouldn't be complicated.

Remember, the more days per week called for and the more complex the routine, the less likely you will be able to stick to it, and the more likely it is to have been designed by and for drug users. Yes, that remark will infuriate a lot of people. Sorry about that. Some drug-free lifters are known to train five days a week, but with very short sessions. But how

Pre-Competition Cycles (continued)

B Day
1. **Trap Bar lift off block.** 4 x 8.
2. **Partial pulls.** 5 x 5.
3. **Heavy rows or pulldowns.** 3 x 8.
4. **Tinkering: curls, calves.**

Tenth week: Max out lifts. Take a break.

Third Cycle
- Simplify—emphasis moves to competition form and performance.
- Go to competition style in all lifts.
- Fewer assistance sets and less "tinkering."
- Drop the reps on the three lifts and increase the number of sets.
- Begin with schemes of 6 x 4 one day and 3 x 6 for top weights the other, working the reps down to threes and fives over the length of the cycle.

You might try a workout at the third and sixth week marks with a weight equal to a tough triple, and do multiple single attempts with it. This is a confidence builder and trains your groove with more or less "opening attempt" poundages.

many days a week anybody trains any lift or body part should be dependent only on recovery capability.

During the second cycle I utilized the power rack even more. Too often this great strength builder is used only as a squat rack. Far too many "instructors" in gyms haven't a clue how to use it. Sometimes you walk in and the locker attendant has towels drying on it.

I set the pins for the squat low so that the boys had to assume the deep position, thighs at parallel or a hair higher, to *begin* the lift. I noticed the gym owner was watching again. He stayed longer this time, grunting his way through a cigar.

I showed 'em that after standing erect, the bar is lowered onto the pins so that the weight is off the lifter briefly between reps. The same method is true for the bench; the pins were set so the bar was just off the chest on full inhale. If no power rack is available, this technique can be done with an extended pause in the bottom position in either movement. Start light, of course (see Chapter 6).

Other common uses for the power rack that we worked in were short lockout movements, and setting one pair of pins above the starting position so the movement could not be locked out. The trainee pushes the weight against the pins for a count of five to ten and then lowers the bar down to the starting pins. All power rack training is tough, and I'd suggest that these exercises not be done more than once a week and then for only six to eight weeks several times a year unless you are a very advanced specimen.

The final cycle was also simple and more or less standard. I'll go into more detail in the last chapter, but it was primarily a rep scheme of five's and three's using contest style. I insisted on proper form throughout the ten months, pauses at the chest on first reps on the bench, and speed emphasis on the lifts through the first two cycles. On deadlift days we'd use sumo style for warm-up sets, just to practice form. We maxed out all lifts at the end of each cycle.

Toward the end of the last two cycles we had a single workout in which we loaded our estimated opening attempt for each lift and tried to do five perfect singles with it.

I've been hearing a lot about "modern Bulgarian training methods" recently. Well, it isn't, and they ain't. Guys were doing ten singles with a constant load for weightlifting training back in the thirties. Sticking with a weight for a high number of low-rep sets has been around and was revived in the sixties on the West Coast as "California sets," mostly using a high percentage of max singles in the 85-90% range.

Doing several heavy low-rep sets of a given lift every day, or even spaced out through the day two or three times is not new. Paul Anderson is known to have done this. It is interesting to watch old routines coming around again, although they are sometimes claimed as new. Old-timers familiar with Rader or McCallum may have tried doing a set of six to ten reps of curls and tricep work every hour or two—while glugging protein shakes—in hopes of adding a permanent half inch to their arms in a few days. I've done this myself with good results. (Many articles have appeared over the years about this idea, always working the arms. Why not other body parts? Seems logical.)

A very recent development called "evolution training" calls for seven to eight short workouts a week with heavy doubles and singles on any given lift, arranged in an exotic scheme based on percentages. The idea that this type of training might work well for many actually seems likely to me, but is tempered by the stone-cold fact that few are likely to get the chance to train this way unless on vacation, independently wealthy or riding a government subsidy.

Ed Coan, perhaps the dominant powerlifter of our time, has advocated long cycles of 5 x 5 and 8 x 3 constant weight rep schemes. I do not recommend this for anybody who has not been training consistently for several years unless he starts down around 60% and builds up. A slight problem is that many commercial gym owners hate this type of routine because it ties up equipment for long periods of time and discourages the less advanced.

When the contest weekend finally rolled around and we were loading gear into my van, the gym owner eased up to me and pressed fifty bucks in small bills into my hand.

"Thought you could use this," he growled, and shambled next door to the deli.

We spent the money on post-meet groceries. The boys came home with a couple of trophies, Class II and III rankings and big ambitions. All their lifts had gone up by 50-70 pounds since Day One. The big boy won his class by five pounds with his last deadlift. The gym owner took me to coffee.

Tried to sell me the gym.

CHAPTER 10

The Stretch Mark Machine

There was an uncomfortable silence when Lope Delk took off his bench shirt and hung it on the upright. A small crowd had been watching out of the corners of their eyes as the "old guy" with the cowboy mustache worked up to 365. Now the rawhide physique with the farmer's tan was bared for all to see. The muscularity was more that of a man who had sweated in oil fields and logging plots than in gyms.

The gang stared in macabre fascination at the network of scars, gouges and stretch marks lacing his torso. Under the right scapula was a four-inch long indentation left by the white pine that had fallen across his back, punctured a lung and partially crippled a leg. The left deltoid carried a suspicious pucker reflecting the effects of Federale gunfire from what a Matamoros, Mexico newspaper described as a "general melee." As in the John Prine song, he had a little shrapnel in his knee, courtesy of the Viet Cong.

On top of this lay roadmaps of stretch marks in the pec-delt tie-in area and under the arm pits over the upper lats. He resembled a high altitude, infrared photo of the South Dakota Badlands. Lope was oblivious to the stares. It would never occur to him to display himself any more than he could understand why anyone would want to do such a thing.

Lope had taken my being in Sacramento as a good excuse for a vacation and a chance to show the blonde 121-pounder some country. That he was the toughest and meanest looking down-from-the-hills hombre to walk into a gym in Sacramento since the Gold Rush meant nothing to Lope, if he was even aware of it. I have known him a long time and believe he assumes everybody picks up similar souvenirs as part of the natural order of things.

I have witnessed some strange happenings and heard some outrageous notions in the forty years I've been around the iron world. But the all-time, world class, "unclear on the concept" award has got to go to the kid who was standing next to me. His eyes were just about popping out of his head, and the expression on his face was mix of awe, hero worship and transcendental envy. He stood transfixed, mouth open, watching Lope work out for the next half hour. Occasionally the kid would turn to the mirror and hold his arms full length over his head and check his armpits.

I was pulling on my sweats to go when the boy sidled over and sat by me.

"Uh, Mr. Kelso, you write for the magazines and know a lot of people and all, well, I was, uh, wondering if you could tell me how to get 'em?"

"Get what?"

"Them." He pointed at Lope.

"Them what?"

"Stretch marks."

"What?"

"I mean, what exercises do I do?"

"WHAT?"

"For stretch marks. Is there a special machine for them, or could I have one made?"

"HAWNH?"

Take it on faith about that last word. That's roughly the sound of the East Texas good ole boy who absolutely does not comprehend what is going on. I felt like Lope's pine tree had landed on me. The look on my face must have scared the lad off. He left me sitting there as I pondered the possibilities. First there was the plate-loading barbell, then power racks and pec-decs, stair climbers, curl bars and squat bars, and next, direct from a post office box in Sacramento—THE STRETCH MARK MACHINE!!

Think of it. A whole new industry waiting for marketing. I figured I'd start with overpriced chrome jobs for the franchise spa chains, followed by heavy-duty models for the iron gyms. Then promo rip-offs from Taiwan at $49.95 for the late cable movie channels. Plus, paint-on stretch marks out of the bottle (washes off with water) to be sold on the same counter with instant suntan solutions. To cap off my career, licensed franchises complete with bonded, blonde technicians in lavender leotards who will help the customer pick a design that is suited to his or her lifestyle and personality (choice of colors optional).

The amount of pain inflicted during treatment will depend on the customer's ability to pay, of course.

Finally, the ultimate culmination: bodybuilding contests with points and special awards categories for "Best Stretch Marks." Think of the women's flights. Boggles the mind.

When I told Lope what the kid had asked I could see the decision to head on back forming in his eyes.

"Is there something in the well water out here? Hell, I'd give him all a' my scars he wants, if I could."

Then Lope fixed a slitted, Clint Eastwood eyeball on the boy for a good thirty seconds.

"Maybe I oughta' arrange for him to have a few for his ownself."

There is a certain kind of stupidity that Lope can't abide, usually centered on another's inability or unwillingness to come in out of the rain. I hustled him on out the door. I glanced back over my shoulder and saw the kid standing there, looking like a four-year-old who had just seen Santa Claus drive by the house without even slowing down.

My guess is that the youngster saw Lope's scars and marks as a badge of manhood that, once obtained for himself, would make him mature and masculine. Not to mention he'd be the first kid on the block to have them. Reminds me of all the teenage soldiers I served with who went out on their first pass and headed straight for the tattoo parlor. They wanted desperately to be considered men. Unfortunately, neither tattoos nor stretch marks will stop bullets or bring instant strength and respect.

I am no expert on this, but as I understand it, stretch marks are caused by extremely rapid growth of muscle or fat deposits under inelastic skin. Women who have borne children often have these marks on their abdomens for much the same reason. Excessive use of stretching movements with heavy weights while overemphasizing pec-delt training is the chief culprit in weight training. Because so many trainees work that area out of all proportion to other body parts, the result is uneven localized growth.

Lope's taut, leathery hide was caused by years of work in the Texas sun and the fact that he has never carried any visible body fat. When he began benching at age 43, his skin could not adjust to the unfamiliar strain or grow with the new muscle. Lope wrote the stretch marks off as the price of doing business. The man has a lot of pride, but no ego, if that makes any sense. He thinks "narcissism" has something to do with Neches River numbweed.

If I could develop a special machine that would get *rid* of stretch marks, I'd become a millionaire and retire. These marks may look impressive to some now, but most older men and women, including myself, would pay big bucks to have them gone. Many do. The marks become more unsightly with age as the underlying tissue atrophies. It's true they are usually harmless, although a few people have developed adhesions that can be quite painful. Ask Lope, if you can find him. He went back to Texas and moved as far back in the woods off the pavement as possible.

So many trainees want to look the part without doing the work necessary to obtain the benefits. I actually knew a guy who went to a clinic and received silicon implants for his pecs. One side didn't take and the lump slid down to his hip. He nearly died from the complications, and the "doctor" was out of business.

There are horror stories going around about the growing number of botched surgical implants, liposuctions and reductive procedures that are performed for cosmetic reasons only, including those done for an expanding group of competitive bodybuilders. A top Mr. Olympia contender was recently accused by rivals of having had his calves implanted. Four hundred-odd pec implant jobs were reported in 1990 alone, mostly among young men age 20 to 30, and costing as much as $6,000!

Who needs this nonsense, and why?

The old definition and purpose of "physical culture" was to enhance health, strength, fitness, athletic ability and—last—image. This seems to be getting turned around. I regard the bodybuilding tradition, both the practice and the competition, as an honorable pursuit. But I am certainly developing some reservations about the bodybuilding scene of today, and "bodybuilding" through surgery and medical procedures goes against my grain. It contradicts everything the physical culture movement in all its aspects has ever stood for.

We haven't reached the point yet where "All, all are vanity," as Preacher Harley might misquote, but it looks like the trend. To compound matters, most gyms, except maybe the fern-bar types, now have two or three yahoos on board (sometimes employees!) whose main motivation is to get humongous in order to intimidate others and who dress like refugees from a leather bar.

Remember, people, image and fantasies don't do one thing for your health, strength, sports prowess or adult career unless maybe you're following in the footsteps of Hulk Hogan. Whatever you may think about pro wrestlers or their "sport," even they have to get in there and *do it*. I know; I used to be one. I hung it up after getting three ribs broken and my nose adjusted in a match with a "predetermined outcome."

Translation: "Fixed." Fixin' me took a while.

I suppose the behavior of the kid who wanted stretch marks can be overlooked or understood, but too many so-called adults fall into similar traps. I probably sound like Preacher Harley here, but looking good, "bad" or imposing is no substitute for striving to be the best and working for genuine achievement.

Lope came by his "badges" honestly, but the person who *seeks* the bizarre and grotesque to bolster his low self esteem would better spend his money on counseling than gym dues and exotic supplements or growth drugs.

It is the freaks in the Iron Game that give the public a bad image of us all.

CHAPTER 11

Resolutions Revisited

I had resolved that nothing that's been alive since the Cretaceous Era could drag me to the New Year's Eve dance, Bench Press contest and Armadillo Bar-B-Que over to Lope Delk's bar out on the Old Kilgore Highway.

I'd been told I had a real good time when I last made that scene, not counting the part about diving twelve feet down in Black's Slough trying to tie a rope around the axle of my '66 Plymouth so Lope could pull it out with the backhoe. On January 2. In front of an ice storm.

Just before sunup on that New Year's Day, we pulled off the road to recycle some beer. We had all just picked out a tree when the old transmission in the "Plimmie" popped into neutral on its own, and the junker merrily rolled down the hill and across the beach with Preacher Harley asleep in the back. We thrashed through the brush and straggled out behind in hot and noisy pursuit.

The car majestically floated on out to the middle of the slough. Preacher's big-eyed face suddenly appeared in the back window and he mouthed a perfect "Holy S—!" He somehow crawled out the window and up on the trunk without turning the car over and sat there white-faced, gasping like a beached carp while the water slowly rose around his collar. A half-dozen empty "supplement" cans surfaced around him and bobbed on the rising bubbles. Then he stood on his tail and made like a paddle wheeler for shore.

Squatlo heard the old bugles call in his somewhat mixed gun dog's genes and swam out and commenced trying to get Preacher by the collar. We were right behind the dog. Ever notice it's semihard to have hysterics and swim all to once? Preacher was trying to swim, fight off the dog, and whack us for getting him into the mess, all at the same time. We all made it on to the beach someway, with Preacher floundering and spouting and muttering about "Triton's Horn" and the faith of fisher folk.

Such were those times. But this visit the redheaded 148-pounder and I had flown into Texas like a Stealth bomber squadron in hopes that we could see the relatives and sneak out again unscathed. Not to be: Lope's got more spies around than the Afghani army, and he and Preacher Harley and Coach Koltuniak were slouched all over the boat dock when we drove up. My wife said a couple of polite "highdys"; I'd forgot she could speak the language, being a Yankee and all, and then she took off up the hill to her mama's like a Girl Scout that had just stumbled on to a biker's bar mitzvah.

Lope wanted to know if she lifted anymore. The redhead had been a fine collegiate lifter before she decided to go to grad school and sent me off to Sacramento to find a job and get set up before she came out.

I told him she'd retired to concentrate on the books, not to mention her disgust at the number of lady lifters who were developing heavier beards than mine from the "supplements" they were taking. Besides, her lats had thickened so much that she couldn't get on those pretty dresses her mama had made her. They knew just who to blame. Me.

Lope pulled out a couple of door passes and told me to be sure to bring her along New Year's Eve and we'd have some fun then. I'd been in the Husband's Union long enough to know better than to even mention it to the lass, so I stuck the passes in my wallet and forgot all about it.

We killed an hour or two doing "old home week" and throwing out treats for the high-fin blue catfish that hung around the dock waiting for lunch to fall in. Three or four good-sized keepers. I promised the boys we'd get together in a few days.

New Year's Eve me and the redhead set out for dinner for two at a high rent restaurant in Jacksonville but when we clanked to a halt, I discovered that the old junker had gone about thirty miles out of the way and pulled up in front of the Scoot 'N Boot. Ever notice how your car sometimes knows where you want to go no matter what you told it in the first place?

The joint hadn't changed much. Screen wire windows all around, the tin barn roof that had been delivered by a tornado, the cable spool patio tables, the fight going on in the parking lot—you know the place.

As we got out of the car, the 148-pounder gave me one of those sweet smiles that men come to know and dread.

"This your idea of a big New Year's celebration with your wife?"

I was indignant. "Honey, these people made me what I am today."

She slammed the car door.

"And what, pray tell, is that?"

"Just one drink, and then we'll go."

"Try to keep the car out of the lake this year, O.K.?"

The seven-foot, 250-pound, ex-Wampus Cat bartender grinned when he saw us.

"Coach Kelso, you done got rich and made Lope famous."

Guess he didn't know how much us big-time Iron Game writers make. Don't ask. Then he started ringing the big church bell behind the bar that the school Prez was still looking for since Lope remodeled the chapel. The employees came running and the regulars crowded in hoping there was gonna' be a fight.

Everyone was there: Coach Koltuniak was wearing his best cowboy outfit and squiring Miss Stotts, the New Age librarian; the blonde 121-pounder was sporting a ring as big as a speed collar and hanging on Lope. LaVonda Sue Braley was arm in arm with Preacher

Harley and the Big Kid from Houston in his college letter jacket and, God help me, there stood the Weight Club hardhead with two waitresses from the malt shop.

I guess he had finally gotten old enough to drink legally. Now he could hang out in bars and brag about his 330 bench despite the fact it hadn't gone up in a two years even though he maxed on it three or four times a week and got his supplements out of a keg.

I took a lot of flack about having gone Hollywood and finally admitted I might have stretched the truth once or twice. The redhead raised an eyebrow and wandered off by the pool tables. Asked a couple cowboys who worked days at Wal-Mart if she might challenge. What the heck, we needed the plane fare back.

The rest of us loaded plates from the trestle table buffet with ribs and a little of this and that. A little fried snapping turtle, a little dollop of turkey "fries," a little 'possum on rice and half a dozen other UFO's (unidentified fried objects): the unmentionable body parts of improbable animals laved with unspeakable sauces. You want exotic? Lope'll give you exotic.

The gang took over a table and settled down to some serious lifting talk. Preacher Harley began pulpiting about me being a "voice from a far land." I think somebody slipped something into his orange Nehi.

The Club hardhead wasn't impressed. He considered me a relic from the days of leopard skin posing tights. Since he had become a college junior after only three years, he regarded himself as an intellectual. He fixed me with a cool gaze and assumed what he thought was a condescending tone.

"Tell me, Mr. Kelso, what is the most important factor in training?"

"Showing up."

"What is the main factor for success at one's first meet?"

"Showing up."

"All right, but seriously, what is the secret of great overall strength?"

"Squats, maybe deadlifts."

He fidgeted. "How should one proceed to widen the shoulders and deepen the chest?"

"Breathing squats."

"What *stack* do you recommend for gaining mass and size?" he shouted.

I poked around in my armadillo fricassee a moment; knowing Lope, it was likely rattlesnake.

"Squats, food and youth; works pretty good."

"WHAT ABOUT THE BENCH PRESS, DAMMIT??!!"

"Twice a week. After squats."

The hardhead jumped up and stomped off to the other end of the bar after recommending a challenging but unlikely exercise for me to go do. Preacher Harley followed after him muttering something about me being a "prophet in his own country." LaVonda fixed on me with her Stonehenge priestess eyes.

"You're being ugly, Mr. Kelso."

Yes, I suppose I was. Playing the bully and I wasn't even on 'roids. Too many holiday electrolytes. I made a resolution to start treating folks better.

I wanted to get out of there before the bench contest started. They wanted me to judge and I wasn't about to red-light anybody in that crowd. Let me set it straight. I've got nothing against the bench press. It's one of the big five or six exercises that everybody needs. But I get a little "flustrated," as they say around Lope's part of the English-speaking world, that three-fourths of all iron heads seem to spend three-fourths of their time on the bench, and wave a hand in passing at the squats, deadlifts, heavy pulls and overhead moves they need to be become truly outstanding.

I found the 148-pounder over on the weight platform with the two cowboys she'd just skunked at eight-ball. The men were grouching about how women "ain't got no business fooling with men's business" and doing deadlift singles to put her in her place. Slamming the bar and making lots of noise. With 255. That's two fifty-five. Pounds. She stepped up and did reps with it until she got bored, put it down and waved 'em good-by.

"Keep it in the yard, boys."

We eased on out the door and turned to watch LaVonda and the seven-foot bartender doing a dance that sure wasn't the "Cotton-eyed Joe." Miss Stotts was explaining Burmese breathing exercises to Coach as they got in his truck. He was breathing pretty good, seemed to me.

"Hey, Kelso," he hollered, "ain't Sacramento up by Amarillo someplace?"

He had to do it. Professional Texan. From Pennsylvania.

The hardhead came slobbering up as I fumbled for the car keys. He was crying and apologizing all the hell over the place and turning my hair white with his breath and saying he knew I was right and how he was gonna' quit drinking so much and get on squats for sure. Well, O.K. I hope he does, and a lot more like him, too.

We're getting in the car when the redhead turns to me.

"Paul, what do you get from these people?"

"Six more articles."

The wise guy writer strikes again. She looked at me for a long moment.

"I miss 'em, too, sometimes."

She was definitely a keeper.

I saw Lope standing in the door as I graveled out to the highway. I held the car on the shoulder as we locked eyes for a moment. Then we shot each other with our forefingers and were gone.

CHAPTER 12

Texas Training Table

What do Texas lifters and trainees eat? They have the same confusion about diet and supplements as everybody else. But Lope and Preacher Harley and the rest of the gang have a few secrets. They don't know much about nutritional science, but they know enough to stick to the three basic food groups: Tex-Mex, Cajun and ranch.

Tex-Mex is simply the world's finest cuisine, and I don't care if that remark harelips every diet gourmet in California. Basic ingredients are beef, chicken, cheese, corn, corn tortillas (white flour tortillas don't get it), beans, peppers of all kinds, lettuce, tomatoes, onions white and green, avocado (talk about an energy food!), eggs, fruits, lime, various spices and sauces, and rice. Margaritas and Tecate beer are optional.

Tex-Mex doesn't have to be greasy or fattening if properly prepared. Most restaurants use low quality, fatty beef and processed cheeses which become runny when cooked. Most hamburger is an aberration. Chopped or cubed round steak or beef roast is just fine. Grass-fed if you can find it. Best prep is not fried, but oven- or stone-baked or grilled.

A little known but marvelous dish is baked kernel corn. Fill a baking dish about two-thirds full of corn, mix in enough chopped red and green bell pepper for flavor, and a little sweet white onion, and cover it over with a mild, white jack or Monterey cheese and a lot of sliced black olives. You might add a light sprinkle of hot spice of your choice. Bake it slow and then enjoy, die, and go to heaven.

Cajun food has had a fit of popularity in the last decade, but most restaurants yuppy it up to the point of nonrecognition. Red beans and rice is a cheap, nutritious delight. I paid $14.95 for a dish of it in an L.A. Cajun cuisine joint five years ago. Figured it cost 'em 95 cents to make it. Real seafood gumbo is almost erotic. Crawfish are hard to come by, but shrimp will do. As Lope would say, "Them groceries is semi-fine." (Use of the word "those" in his circle brands one an outsider.) The secret to a great gumbo is okra. This strange veggie is not real popular in the U.S. outside the South because of its somewhat slimy texture when boiled or steamed. Fried or sliced into a stew, it's great. It is one of the most nutritious plants on earth.

Ranch food is both awful and wonderful. Corn bread from scratch is great; the ready-mix stuff pales in comparison. How well I remember my lanky, red-haired father and his Uncle Dub pouring sorghum syrup or molasses on to their plates and whipping real butter into it till the mess became a paste to be spread on the sweet corn bread or soda biscuits. Breakfast on the Sunshine Hill farm was that and eggs fried till the edges crinkled lacy brown, sometimes fried chicken basted with peach preserves and slices of fried onions, green tomatoes and potatoes and fried apples with brown sugar and lean ham—the farm had the skinniest and best tasting pigs in creation—and, oh yes, grits.

Grits are used like rice or potatoes. They are intended as a vehicle for whatever you want to put on them. Made from white corn, they can be eaten like oatmeal (put that on your list, too, but forget the instant drool), covered in butter and salt and pepper or mixed with ham gravy. Gnomish Uncle Dub, half bobwire and bobcat, would break a raw egg over the hot grits and stir it all in. Real grits are far more nutritious than most instant cereals, so look for the genuine stuff.

And the coffee. Right now go out to the kitchen and gather up all the plastic percolaters, glass carafes and drip-dry contraptions and haul them down to the boat dock and drop them off the end. They'll make good cover for the fingerlings next spring. Then drive over to the nearest old-time hardware store, if there still is one in your area, and buy a gallon or bigger size speckled blue and white enamel old-style by-god coffee pot.

Fill it with water and bring it to a boil. Throw in a couple of handfuls of regular ground coffee. Break a raw egg and drop the shells in the pot (some insist on the shells of brown eggs that have dried in the oven). Add Grandma's "peench" of salt. Let it boil again till it's done. After about two weeks you'll have figured out the process and the amounts and will have great coffee. Warning: let it cook or sit too long and you can use it to stain the furniture.

The raw egg? Put it in the grits, give it to the dog—or glug it.

Maybe I'm out of order here, but I'm including barbecue in with the ranch list. Bar-B-Q is maybe a mix of Spanish and black culture in origin. Beef or pork, if lean, fixed right, meaning on the dry side, with a homemade sauce rather than that bottled stuff which may be made by engine lube brewers, served with chili beans, potato salad, cole slaw, giant dill pickle slices, white bread and a bottle of Shiner Bock beer is beyond description.

Wait a minute. White bread? Yeah, I know, it's a no-no, but there is simply nothing better to sop up the leavin's. And, it's sacrilegious to use anything else.

Chili with hamburger as a base is often too greasy. Never use pork. I have eaten a decent chicken chili, but regard it as a curiosity. Real chili was made with cow or buffalo or deer meat. Real range buffalo is very lean and very high protein, altogether superior to beef, but has a strong taste. Hybrid "beefalo" may be more palatable but much of it and the "100% genuine buffalo meat" now on the market are now being raised on the standard diet fed to beef cattle, thus raising the fat content, altering the nutritional value and blanding up the taste.

Chili is not a traditional Mexican dish, but an invention of the southwestern frontier, with a little help from the local Indians, and probably did not contain meat in its original form. Arguments can be heard at chili "cook-off" contests whether meat and/or beans should be included.

I do it all. Take maybe two pounds of cubed round or, if forced, brown it with chopped onions and bell pepper, and then drain off the grease. Put the meat in a big kettle, dump in a can or two of ranch-style beans, at least one (gasp) can of tomatoes (go light on these at first, you can always add more), and shake in a pack and a half of chili-mix spices. Cook it slow so the spices have time to work.

Original ingredients may be better, but my way is quicker. Serve it in a bowl with lots of corn chips on hand to scoop with, or pour it over rice and stir it in. Make tacos. Good with crumbled-up Saltine crackers mixed in, too. Should feed four to five folks. Filling, tasty, nutritious, yes, but such fare may make you socially unacceptable. Do I have to explain that?

It's worth it.

By the way, just as nearly every farmer in the upper Midwest in America has a pint of apricot brandy under the seat of his pickup truck to help him get through the winters, many back country southwesterners carry a can or two of tomatoes. They are just great as a thirst quencher.

But the all time best was, and is, chicken fried steak. Oh, Lordy. Look, this isn't quantum physics. Take a big ole slab of half-inch thick round steak, pound the heck out of it with one of those corrugated hammers (a ballpeen works pretty good), then make the same kind of batter you would if you're gonna' fry chicken. Be sure there's an egg in it. Black pepper. Soak the steak in it for half an hour. Then roll it in flour. Fry it up pretty crispy. Then make a thick cream gravy from the leavings. Pour it over the steak, and the mashed potatoes, the biscuits, and anything else in sight. Side dishes might include turnip greens, cold beets and cole slaw. Raw sliced turnip or rutabaga is a great munchie with a little salt. Rhubarb cobbler for dessert, and you're home free.

And not least, catfish and crappie and young bass, fried or baked, never mind, devour till you drop, yes, that'll do.

I know many, if not most, of the the current generation of health food adherents and gurus reading this are appalled. Well, take a Valium, folks. Nobody would suggest that the above be followed exclusively. In fact, my old pen-pal, Master's class lifter Jumpin' Jersey Joe Pyra, disagrees completely. He insists the three basic food groups are beer, pierogi and kielbasa.

These Texas diets or menus evolved out of necessity from what was and, in some cases, is available. They beat hell out of what the majority of the American people eat today. And, like it or not, they were established into the folkways and the traditions because they were needed.

Texan and Southern farmers and ranchers put in long, hard, "can't-see to can't-see" days and didn't worry about their cholesterol counts. They needed the calories to do their tasks and yet stayed lean. They worked off the heavy breakfast calories and the carcinogens from the barbecue and lived into their eighth, ninth and sometimes tenth decades, like my folks, who are absurdly long-lived.

Of course, if you eat this way without exercising or physical labor you can expect to look like an insurance agent in Shreveport who spends too much time in the night spots over on the Bossier City strip.

We've all read about the California bodybuilding stars who reportedly live on seven-grain muffins and egg-whites and yogurt with crushed strawberries as part of their "superior lifestyle." Such stuff is good food and useful for paring down for a physique show or maintaining lean bodyweight for a lot of activities. But the number of iron heads who have used such "diets" to gain 50-100 lbs. and triple or quadruple their strength during their training and competitive careers could be gathered together in the back booth of the Scoot 'N Boot.

Like any diet, it's the balance of activity versus intake that makes the final determination, and in my personal view, we are just now beginning to learn what the questions are on weight control, not the answers. If you are going to try to become a giant, then learn to eat like one. You've got to have carbs and calories as well as protein and other nutrients to gain on a heavy exercise program. Frontier country ideas and recipes can make it easier, and a heckuva lot less boring.

CHAPTER 13

First Meet Follies: A Primer

There's an old saw about all good things coming to an end. Good or not, we're getting there.

My career and circumstance took me far from Pine Woods College, and even from America. Last I heard Lope and the blonde 121-pounder were settled in the woods, Preacher Harley taught at a seminary, LaVonda was making films in France, the Club hardhead owned a couple hamburger stands, the Big Kid from Houston became an architect, and Miss Stotts and Coach Koltuniak had two kids.

The redheaded 148-pounder packed her gear bag and changed gyms, so to speak. A cliché in the sixties was that a true test of love was being willing for the loved one to be free. I still buy that. All good things . . .

Me? I went to Japan to teach English. I've been lucky enough to travel all over Asia, covering contests and sending back articles to *PLUSA*, *IRONMAN* and *Hardgainer*. Even finished the shrug book. But I've had a connection to home and to the weight world there through letters from friends, old and new.

Many are from people who want to compete. From the letters I get there are probably thousands of beginners and intermediate trainees who are thinking about it, but don't have a clue how to get started, how to prepare, who to contact or what to do when they get there. The comments in this chapter are primarily for fledgling powerlifters; but much of what I say is basic advice that applies to weightlifting and bodybuilding as well.

When the Big Kid from Houston asked me at the beach how come I didn't take the Wampus Cats to a meet, I couldn't think of one good reason not to. Other than we weren't ready, were disorganized, had no suits and such, and were stone flat broke. Luckily, we had a club and a local fanatic, me, to push things together and keep it going.

But what if there is no club or school team to provide support for the neophyte, of any age, who wishes to enter his first meet? Many are training in the exile of home gyms and confusing themselves monthly by reading half a dozen magazine articles which appear to offer contradictory advice. Others lift with friends who all have a cousin who trains a certain sure-fire way, or at the local "health club" where the house ego-pumper passes on information designed to support his own version of how great he is.

This fellow puts off entering meets because he wants to get his bench up to 400 first. He never has entered and never will because his ego cannot risk defeat. Yet he has no trouble advising other would-be lifters as to what they should do. Compound this with confusion around selecting which organization to join, and the newcomer is truly in the iron wilderness. I'm going to make some recommendations on how to overcome these problems, big and little, and hope that I'll start getting more letters from people who have gotten off dead center and had some genuine success.

The first thing is to get in touch with somebody who has actual knowledge of what is happening. Look through the magazines for the pages that list upcoming contests, find the names of the promoters and contest chairmen in your area, and write them for information. Better yet, call! Ask them if they can send a list of contests scheduled for the year and the scoop on the organizations they represent.

Get the rules of both the game and the outfit and learn them. Make a tour of the gyms in your area and talk to the owners and some of the local competitors, if you can find them. Read all the flyers on the walls. Get the names and addresses of the honchos who are trying not to go broke while attempting to develop your sport in their area.

Some of the folks you run into will be surly, steroid-rage jerks, including a few gym owners who don't have time for "mullets" like you. Unless they think they can sell you some muscle junk. Most are nice people who are willing to help anybody trying to get started. Don't give up. You may find the regional fanatic living nearby your home. Seek out the right people for your own area. Investigate several groups and shop around for the one that suits you best. How will you know? What's the difference?

Well, many of the alphabet soup lash-ups who claim to be the "World" this or the "American" that, no matter how well-intentioned, just simply ain't what they advertise. The scene is becoming like pro wrestling where "world champions" of half a dozen different outfits appear on several TV channels nightly. The new competitor, if that's you, absolutely does not need to get involved in the political wars between the organizations. The establishment of so many new groups has been caused by differences of opinion among veteran competitors and new-on-the-scene promoters with the older outfits over rules, drug-usage and testing, authorized gear, international participation, TV rights, personality clashes and flat-out greed.

You don't care.

Not yet.

Whether you are in high school or college, in your teens or in your sixties, I suggest you get in touch with one of the major groups, all of which have considerable experience staging contests at every level. Most organizations have held meets for all categories, some of them fine affairs, but the majors hold more contests over a wider geographical area and are likely to have one coming up at any given time.

When you get the flyers and schedules, take a close look at what's offered. A meet calling itself the "Tri-State Monster Open" may sound like an intergalactic showdown in the magazine announcement and scare you off at first. Then you notice down in the fine print it has divisions for High School or Teens, Novices, Class III and under, Class II, Elite, Open, Masters rank or Masters over 40, Pure, Clean, Two-years Clean, Closed, Invitational, Drug Tested Polygraph or Drug Tested Urinalysis or both, Lefthanded, Methodist or Republican.

If you are an eighteen-year-old high school 181-pounder who totals 1050 in the gym, this can be confusing. You do *not* want to enter the Open class first time out (unless it's a very small contest—used to be you could sometimes win a very impressive-sounding title simply because you were the only guy to show up in your class, but you can't count on that happening these days). Find a contest with a High School flight, if you can, because the Teen flight at the Asparagus Day Extravaganza may include 20-year-olds, depending on the rules of the sanctioning group.

No matter what your age, Class II (USPF) and under meets are pretty safe, as are Novice and Collegiate contests in any organization, but there are land mines. Novice often means that anyone can enter who has never placed first in any contest. This can allow some hellacious competitors to sneak into your flight. This happens in bodybuilding as well. College upperclassmen may be nearing Junior National or higher qualification and might bend your freshman beanie propellor down around your ears.

Over-40 hopefuls shouldn't give it a second thought. Most contests you enter you'll be treated like a hero just for showing up. But be warned: While large over-40 contests are broken down into age groups such as 40-44, 45-50, etc., many are decided by a pound-for-pound bodyweight formula, and every jurisdiction now has several silverbacks who can play havoc with the curve. Enter anyway—you owe it to yourself.

The point is to find a meet with a division that suits you best for where your progress is currently. On the other hand, unless you are really a "phenom," you should not be concerned about winning the first several times out. Compete and learn and look to the future. Once in a great while, some benefactor of the sport will stage a "developmental" contest for beginners. If you find such a show, jump in!

After going through all the materials and talking to everybody you can corner, pick a contest three or four months off and enter it *now*. Make a commitment. Invest the money. Don't wait till the last minute and end up rushing around in a panic getting your act together. This will also stave off the urge to back out at the last minute.

One of the most common and useless phenomenoms in all of the iron sports, and many others, I suspect, is the strange shuffle of the competitor who procrastinates until the deadline in hopes his total or condition will be high enough to justify entering. It may never be. This person is just a trophy hunter with little gumption for the long haul toward true success. He's looking for a set up. The quick fix. Sadly, there are a lot of cherry-picking veterans playing this charade as well as excuse-making wannabees. As you are an ethical sportsman with legitimate motivation, that's not your problem. Right?

So, what do you do in the meantime? Here's your list:

1) *Go see a contest.* Many enter without ever having seen one! Study the techniques of competitors whose body proportions are most like your own. Volunteer to be a spotter or to load weights or sell programs. You'll be astonished how much you can learn, and it will hold down the first-meet jitters when it's your turn to get out there and set up for your

opening appearance. Walking into the madhouse of any kind of contest to compete cold can unnerve anybody and is just dumb.

2) *Get your gear.* Squat suit, belt, shoes, bench shirt, posing briefs, or whatever—start collecting right away. Be sure they are legal and within the rules of the organization running the contest. The requirements may vary from one outfit to the next. Nothing could be worse than blowing months of preparation, entry fees and travel expenses by being disqualified from competing because your suit is illegal or your belt is a centimeter too thick or the heels on your shoes are too wide. I've seen it happen.

3) *Try your gear.* Practice each lift in your gear at least once a week for six weeks before the meet. Equipment can change your groove and may effect your choice of opening lifts.

4) *Get help.* Find an experienced lifter or team to hook up with for the contest. You could use some advice. Don't go alone even if you have to take your mom. Have some-body there to make sure you don't miss a turn and to help with your suit and wraps. A good "gopher" can save the contest for you.

5) *Master your wraps.* Learn to roll and tie knee-wraps like a combat nurse way before the meet. Have an extra pair, pre-rolled, on hand.

6) *Plan.* Select your opening and second lift poundages several weeks in advance. A common rule of thumb is to open with a weight that can be done for a solid three reps in training. Experienced lifters figure this to be approximately 87-90% of possible max. The second attempt is 95-97% and the third is 102% or more. This varies depending on how you feel in the warm-up room. Why start so low? To overcome jitters and to get a safe lift in past the judges and get on the scoreboard. You must get in one lift of each type to total.

New lifters fail for many reasons, but the most common by far is starting too high and wasting attempts. I have seen lifters max out the night before the contest because they couldn't make up their minds what to open with! Does this sound familiar?

The second common reason for failure is not knowing the rules governing platform procedure. Third is not practicing the lifts in training according to *the rules of the organi-zation staging the contest you have entered.* Don't wait until the meet to start pausing at the chest during the bench, breaking parallel in the squat or stabilizing the lift at completion before racking it or putting it down. Remember, the rules may vary from one outfit to the next, especially in the bench.

7) *Stop maxing out.* Entire articles have appeared many times about training for the first meet. Let's keep it simple; try max attempts only once every 10-12 weeks during regular training. Veterans rarely attempt a *true* max except at contests. Reduce reps from six to eight to four to six over the months and increase poundages as you go. Once a month do a light, high-rep day with about 50% of your true max. Don't be afraid to add an extra day or two of rest if your body tells you to.

Remember, the more rigid a scheduled program that you see published, the more likely it is that the author assumes you're on drugs—or don't have anything else to do.

Plan to test max yourself to about 95% six or seven weeks before the show, take a few days off and then resume with sets of fives and threes.

The closer you get to the fateful day, do fewer assistance exercises and none at all the last three weeks, except for some waist work and a few sets of upper back pulls. Don't make a lot of changes in your program in the two to three months before a contest unless you are training like "Mr. Wonderful." Get down to basics. Get plenty of rest. Stop training the deadlift eight to ten days before the meet, the squat six and the bench four days out. Some find a light workout of all three lifts with about 50% of max two to three days prior to the contest is an excellent way to keep the edge.

A minority of coaches disagree with all the above. They, like Louie Simmons, believe that a lifter should maintain his volume of poundage lifted right up to a few days before the meet. One gauges exercise weight and projected meet openers not with near-max percentages, but rather on an increasing level of total poundages lifted during the workout. Lighter weights in the 65-75% range are utilized, started slow and then driven through to completion (see Chapter 2, pause, slow transition and explosion). Hatfield named the technique "compensatory acceleration."

Whatever you call it, Louie's methods are not all that different from the old, constant weight, sets and reps schemes of weightlifters, or Coan's 8 x 3's. Like the man said, "There is nothing new in weight training." Louie claims his method is less stressful than the common peaking method now popular among most powerlifters.

In contrast, Dr. Ken Leistner has reported his lifters having good results by keeping to their regular, all-out high intensity, low set and high rep workouts up to a few days before a contest. Is the poundage volume all that different? Stress? Anticipating recovery time is probably the key.

I predict the above ideas will trigger the "Great Debate" of the next few years. I agree that acceleration training works, but suggest it be worked into established programs. The big majority of champions are doing quite well as they are, thank you very much, but prophets are often proven right, in the end.

8) *Eat right.* There is no area in all sports with more conflict of opinion, wild claims and pressure to experiment without real information. My advice? Good solid FOOD first and quality vitamins. Then, if you must, beef liver tabs and/or a good protein powder and maybe a "shotgun" metabolic drink before and after workouts. My experience with inosine, dibencozide and diosgenin is that after an initial boost the body adapts to them. Others have suggested their use should be staggered over time to prevent such accommodation. Another school of thought, exemplified in the writings of Dr. Ken Leistner, suggests that all supplements are pretty much a waste of time. If you are not eating right, they are a waste of time—and money. I once picked up a seven dollar bottle of amino "assets" and calculated the product as having the same nutritional value as a dollar's worth of eggs!

The best result I ever obtained from any compound on a short-term basis was by starting a cycle of a diosgenin-based product three weeks before a planned three lift max-out day. Rumor has it that the stuff, now off the market, may have included a testosterone. I had a great session; it may or *may not* have been from the supplement. There were a lot of factors; I was on a great cycle, was well rested, stress free, in love, and was, for once, untroubled by old injuries.

What about steroids and other regulated wonder drugs and compounds? I would prefer that everybody reach their maximum natural development and strength before they consider using them. Then decide if it's worth it and whether you can get away with it, both personally and in competition. My personal opinion is that it is too risky on the first count and unethical on the second. A third consideration is that many compounds are banned by the organizations and some are flat illegal. If that last doesn't get your attention, you really do have a problem.

Some start drugs almost as soon as they begin training on the grounds that they aren't "genetic naturals" and need the juice to catch up. Any veteran coach can tell you about the ordinary beginner who blossoms naturally beyond anybody's expectations with regular training methods. Give yourself a chance before considering giving yourself a dubious boost.

Yes, some respected authorities believe steroids and other compounds are helpful and not harmful to athletes if administered under properly controlled conditions. My problem is in being convinced that proper control is possible. Many experimental programs are conducted on campuses using batches of students as "control groups." As a former Director of Student Affairs at a college, I can tell you that controlling what students do, eat, drink or take when out of sight is impossible.

"College control group" is an oxymoron.

All the rationalizing by users, sellers and popular gurus will not overcome the fact that steroids are high risk for causing cancers and failure of internal organs. The list of the prematurely departed grows longer. Steroid "rage" and personality and psychological problems are being confirmed by a growing number of studies.

The National Institute of Mental Health reported in late '93 that a short-term low-dose study of male volunteers showed that steroids can quickly alter mood and behavior. "We found signicant increases . . . of distractibility, irritability and energy level, with trends for an increase in anger, violent feelings, insomnia and fatigue."

I'm no scientist, but I'd add paranoia. That's all American men need, more drugs to enhance our fragile male egos and boost our macho, comic book and bad guy outlaw self-images. The effect on women is perhaps too early to ascertain, although lowered voices and facial hair are reported, along with the distension and alteration of external sexual structures. Now, get this, please: These changes in women appear to be nonreversible!

Be extremely careful about mixing and experimenting with compounds whose side effects are not known or predictable.

Damn sure don't mix 'em with booze!

What works for one may work "on" another.

Another risk is that guy in the locker room or the parking lot who wants to sell goodies to you. Not only is what he selling likely to be illegal, the stuff's often bogus or dangerous. I'm also not real crazy about the gym owner who sells them to his members or the high school football coach who gives them to the boys, usually not telling them what they are, claiming they're "special" vitamins.

A California gym owner was arrested a few years ago after $400,000 worth of steroids and etc. were seized from his apartment. He claimed, according to the media, that they were for his own use. Excuse me? This fellow was reported to have made several inspirational talks in the schools *against* steroid use prior to this. Can you believe it?

I also remember reading about that time that the income of the average private gym owner doubled or tripled between 1975 and 1985. I realize we've had a nationwide iron boom, especially in bodybuilding, but is there anyone out there who can assure me that what I'm thinking isn't true?

Several high school football coaches were busted in the last few years for giving their players steroids. I have little sympathy for them, if guilty. The desire to win is one thing; enhancing a coaching career by putting the players at risk is another. The astonishing thing to me in these cases was that the players' fathers often backed the coach!

Shortly before this book went to press, a powerlifting group that believes steroid use is a matter of individual freedom announced a contest featuring two divisions, one to be drug tested and the other with no testing. Just what does that tell a new lifter? As I've responded before: "Hawnh!?"

Supplements or drugs, don't *you* spend your money without clear knowledge of what you're getting and what the product is supposed to do and any possible side effects it may cause.

9) *A couple of comments.* By the time you have gotten your battle gear together, paid your dues and fees and bought a minimum of supplements, you will have spent close to three or four hundred dollars, or more. MUCH more, if you fall into some of the ads I've seen recently. That's a good reason to make a commitment to yourself to give your chosen game an extended chance.

I'll probably get a lot of flack for this next statement. I do not believe that cycle training based on percentages is effective for the vast majority training for a first meet or for the teen or relatively new trainee who is rapidly improving. It works great for the veteran whose gains are hard to come by. The new guy simply does not have the experience to gauge his progress. Unless you find a great coach by next Tuesday, wait until after your first contest when you have a better idea of your real capabilities. One young fellow I know bought a computerized six-month training schedule set up to percentages of his max lifts that lined out sets, reps and poundages. He gave it up after a few months because it was holding him back!

10) *"But what will I do if I bomb out?"* The saddest thing in sports, short of career-ending injury, is the first-timer who fails to total or is beaten so badly that he or she is dream-crushed and never enters again. It happens far too often. Make a personal commitment when you send in your first application that you will enter three meets, no matter what. This will guarantee giving yourself a fair shot.

The Wampus Cats had their share of failures and disappointments. They won only one first place trophy in two years. They didn't do badly for college freshmen and sophomores lifting against four-year schools and all-comers in the big Opens. By their fourth meet they were a cocky bunch of tough little veterans who were proud of their seconds and thirds and fifths. The new kids gawked at *them*.

So don't get discouraged. You'll get there.

I've been assuming you are getting antsy to get going but afraid you'll make a fool of yourself. You may have dreams of winning, or reservations about taking the big step to enter until you can total 1500. What are you waiting for? Enter! Meet experience is worth a year of workouts. Put all the extraneous considerations aside. *Lift for yourself.* It is chancy that you will place, much less win, in your baptismal effort. It does happen but very few can walk in and blow everybody out of the hall the first time out. You are there to learn.

Which leads me to Kelso's first principle of Iron Game competition: SHOW UP!

You will never make greater progress in your career than that made during and immediately after your first contest!

You learn the rules, how to time warm-ups and to react to judges' instructions and commands. You'll experience the initially confusing order, the rhythm of the meet, and getting wraps on and off in a hurry. Dealing with clocks, scorers, and weight selection, will become second nature. You will watch and talk to so many experienced lifters and learn so much and get so fired up, you'll think your squat suit is going to burst. And, if you are like 95% of all first-timers, you will leave the meet lamenting, "I didn't know, I could have done more." You will, too, in that second contest which you will be planning for even before you get home.

Kelso's Laws

These "laws" are not necessarily original with me. Some are so obvious that only the brain dead wouldn't think of them at some point in their training. I've used most of these in published articles at one time or another and some have appeared in the works of others as well as in mine.

Case in point: "Less is more." What it describes in weight training is the odd fact that as one advances in age and strength, gains can continue by reducing the number of sets performed and the number of workouts per week. You don't have to do endless sets and keep a cot in the gym.

Far too many trainees waste years in pursuit of the perfect program and never make real gains until they simplify their routines. Some true

Kelso's Laws

1. Twenty sets (or less) per body; not per body part.
2. There is no one correct way to train.
3. It is useless to train for definition, shape or separation until you have some muscles to define, shape or separate.
4. Showing up is the first rule for success in training or competition.
5. What works for one may not work for another.
6. What works for one may work "on" another.
7. Eat to gain, or don't bother to train.
8. It's not how you train, it's what you're training for.
9. It's not what you train with, it's how you train with it.
10. "Less is more." Stick with 1. except in special circumstances.

Kelso's Corollary

Anyone who thinks he knows all the answers in training doesn't know what the questions are.

"hardgainers" can only trigger growth by using intense workouts of two to four *sets!!* But generally, it means short, determined workouts staying close to the basics and aiming for steady progression in reps and/or poundages.

See Kelso's Law 1. above.

Competition Training

This section discusses the most common approaches to pre-meet PL training: the basic "heavy and light" system, and "three days a week" training (see box). These have been used by more people over the last ten years than any other. They have many variations.

Rotation of Routines (see also Chapter 6): If you plan three separate workouts, you might set them up like this, three times a week: Monday—A; Wednesday—B; and Friday—C.

Five times in two weeks (over four weeks): Week 1: A-B-C; Week 2: A-B; Week 3: C-A-B; Week 4: C-A;

Some training one lift per day, as in the "three days a week" program, also believe that the bench press can be trained more often than the other lifts. A month's schedule might look like this, training three days a week:

Squat—Bench—Deadlift
Bench—Squat—Bench
Deadlift—Bench—Squat
Bench—Deadlift—Bench

T his structure will allow three intensive squat and leg workouts, two heavy DL days and one light, and three heavy bench days and three light in one month. Frankly, I found it best to skip the last BP day of the month to rest, and then start in again with the squat the following Monday. This program has built in rest periods and allows for considerable assistance movements. But, *it is not for beginners!* I'd do six months of basics first, if just starting out.

Yes, some train five days a week on complicated schedules. Hiro Isagawa, six-times world champ and multiple world record holder for the bench, and internationalist Tokiharu Maeda, both of Japan, set it up this way for many years: five bench days, three squat days,

Competition Training

1. **Basic Heavy and Light System.** Train twice a week.

First Day
Squat; bench.
Many do rows or pulls after bench.

Second Day
Deadlift; moderate bench and squat. Heavy DL day is every other week.

Keep the assistance exercises to a minimum. "Mr. Wonderful" workouts will work against a lifter eventually. My "twenty sets or less" law works pretty well here.

2. **Three Days a Week** (this is a growing trend).

Monday: **Deadlift.**
Wednesday: **Squat.**
Friday: **Bench.**

A fourth workout on Saturday might be light bench and other "tinkering." Numerous arrangements are possible.

and two deadlift sessions over a two-week period. Their workouts on any day were about an hour or less in length. Such training is for advanced people and is an individual choice.

Training to a "peak" for a contest: A common pattern for a three- or four-month cycle is to begin with a month of sets of eight to ten reps (more reps for the high bar squat); six to seven weeks of 5 x 4-6 (a few do 6-8 x 3); and a final four to five weeks of fives and threes while shutting off assistance work almost entirely as the meet approaches. See also Chapter 9, for further discussion and alternative methods.

What about bodybuilding? I love to watch a top bodybuilding show. Heck, checking out the audience is worth the price of the ticket! You know you're not there for a PTA meeting the second you walk in, surrounded by folk who are certain that they are not mere mortals, everybody bronzed and bigger than life, their clothing styles imported from another galaxy. The bronzed, dazzling women you know for sure didn't ever come from your home town.

Baffling to me is that the competitor I pick for first usually places fifth, and the hunk who wins is somebody I've completely overlooked. The standards seem to change arbitrarily year to year. I doubt I'll ever be reconciled to watching an underweight, defined, separated specimen with veins like a nest of green racer garden snakes beat out a guy who actually has some muscle. I don't get it.

The politically influenced decisions I've seen made me want to heave right on the judges' table. But any "sport" that has intangible factors or "style" points is subject to that kind of crappola. If you're determined to get in there and take your chances, there's a few things to think about.

Training for competition bodybuilding is a subject unto itself and could take up a full book, or a hundred books. "All the bodies now featured in physique magazines or books have been built by high volume, split training" is a common statement in those publications. This is not exactly true; many, if not most, of those champs spent years on heavy, basic routines similar to those in this book. The "finishing" routines came later or were interspersed as contests approached.

The magazine physiques are also very advanced, genetically blessed specimens that meet the current competition standards. That far too many of those bodies have been built, or at least enhanced, with the use of steroids and other dubious chemical compounds is not often mentioned.

Yes, they are a fact of life in the higher levels of bodybuilding and, sadly, have been invasive in Olympic-style weightlifting for over three decades. Their use has been and is widespread in powerlifting. Just as you can now compete successfully without steroids in several powerlifting organizations (there is a definite trend away from drugs in that sport), there are several growing "natural" or clean bodybuilding groups.

I am bemused and somewhat befuddled by the assumption by so many in the gyms that "everybody is doin' it," that steroid use is not only acceptable but the common order of things. The excuses are uncannily like those of grass-smokers and other types of "heads" who believe that non-users and anti-drug authorities are not "with it" and that it is therefore not only O.K. to beat the system but somehow "in" to do so. A common rationale is that it is their right to use such drugs as a matter of personal choice.

Along with "how much can you bench," the usual locker room questions are "what'cha' using" and "how do you mask it?" A few cynical correspondents suggest to me that the drug testing procedures in place in bodybuilding are structured as public relations "beards" to fool the gullible and to allow the competitors to do as they please. I sincerely hope this isn't true.

What is true is that most (to be kind about it) pro-bodybuilders are almost certainly "on" something. The system for qualifying for higher levels of competition requires building a pro-type body to advance. The pressure to be a user is nearly irresistible to the person trying to get into the money.

The term "drug-free bodybuilder" has become an oxymoron to those on the highest levels. As a rising star touring Japan recently told me, "Hey, man, this is show business."

Unfortunately, or not, as one may see it, he's correct. Bodybuilding has moved away from the old emphasis on health, strength and ability, and has become "bodybuild-ing," a *performance art*, rather than a true sport. It is a form of show business. Well, O.K., if that's what a person chooses. Why do it is another question. But the growing tendency of bodybuilding shills to belittle weightlifters and powerlifters and tout bodybuilders as superior is uncalled for and self-defeating.

Why compare apples and oranges? Maybe competition bodybuilding should stop trying to justify itself as a sport and just be what it is and quit apologizing for itself and bickering with iron heads with different goals.

As I have said, I hope that every new trainee will use the methods described in this book or other basic training methods for several years so that an idea of his or her potential may be honestly assessed. It is *not* true that anyone can become a "Mr. Wonderful"; it *is* true that if you don't have "that look" fairly early in life, you probably never will. Be honest with yourself.

For a new trainee to jump into "Mr. Wonderful" routines and begin gulping down pills like M&M's is just stoo-puhd. One leading magazine recently published a "begin-ners" routine under the byline of a very famous name, calling for a three-times-a-week, *fifty* set, full body workout, using a lot of 5 x 5's. I. Don't. Under. Stand. That.

Many have been doing a "three days on, one day off" split, choosing several body parts a day. That's a little over five workouts a week in a month. Well, guess what? Do the math on that type of routine. It comes out that each body part is worked a hair over three times in two weeks, if you can stick to the schedule. I like my way better for people on the way up. Four to six short full body workouts in two weeks. If you have to miss a workout, and you will sometimes, your entire schedule isn't blown. You get hormone release more often, achieve your potential (drug free) mass and size quicker, and can then go to concentrated split routines for contest preparation.

Concentrating your efforts for eventual bodybuilding competition without getting too far from the principles of this book can be done by splitting your training into two routines. Rather than the full body programs I push for general training, upper body and lower body days could be mapped out. Or you could choose to do a selection of body parts one day and the rest the next. There are many well-known ways to organize such a split, so I'm not suggesting anything new. But how do you handle such a program?

You can train each body part three times in two weeks without training five times a week. I'm aiming at regular folks who have jobs, can't, or don't want to train four to six days a week and do wish to proceed drug-free. Here is how I proceeded over twenty years ago. My A Day was chest, shoulders, traps, biceps and a little waist. B Day was thighs, back, triceps and calves. I did some waist work both days and a lot on off days.

I did six to seven sets each for chest, shoulders and back, eight to ten for thighs, four sets each for biceps and triceps and four to five for calves. Neither day was more than 26 sets nor more than one-and-one-half hours in length. The program looked something like this and is only a suggestion: Monday—A, Wednesday—B, Friday—A; Monday—B, Wednesday—A, Friday—B.

There is no point in trying this program unless you have already gained significant size from the basics. It may seem like a lot of work to some and not enough to others. Three or four rest days are built for each body part. Begin with moderate weights and even fewer sets if you wish, so you can work into the entire program while maintaining good form and a steady pace. This type of training would be useful in preparing for "clean" contests. I stayed on this program for almost six months and did not lose much from my single lift ability. I did become "prettier" than I had ever been.

So much so that one of the partners at the gym urged me to plan to enter a local bodybuilding

Bodybuilding Competition Training

A Day

Chest:
Bench press: 3 x
Incline DB press, or parallel bar dips: 2 x
Flyes or pullovers: 2 x
Shoulders:
Overhead press: 3 x
Side lateral or upright row: 2 x
Traps:
Standing shrug: 2 x
Biceps:
Barbell curl: 2 x
Concentration curl: 2 x
Waist work: 4 x

B Day
Thighs:
Squats: 4 x
Stiff-leg DL or leg curl: 2 x
Leg press: 2 x
Extensions: 2 x
Back:
Chins, rows, pulldowns (your choice): 5-6 x
Kelso shrug: 1-2 x
Rear delt lateral: 2 x
Triceps:
Close grip bench: 2 x
Seated pressdowns: 2 x
Calves:
Donkey: 2-3 x
Seated: 2 x

All sets were 6-8 reps except flyes, pullovers and stiff-leg DL or leg curls, which were 10-12. Waist, calves were 15. A Day is 24 sets and B Day is 26.

show four months in the future. He'd take over as my coach, increasing workouts to five days a week—and—supply me with just the right amount of Dianobol to harden my look and maintain size as I cut up. I told him I'd think about it over the weekend.

The following Monday, the man found me training with renewed dedication— over on the lifting platform, doing hang snatches.

CHAPTER 14

Requiem for a Time

We had a few lines out. It was that best time of day in summer a year or so ago, 'bout a half-hour after sunset, and the grey light would linger afterwards till nearly ten o'clock. The high-fin blue cats and maybe a crappie or two could be expected to volunteer for dinner. It wasn't important, one way or another.

Preacher Harley lay flat-out back up the dock a few feet, his hands in a prayerful attitude, holding a tall-boy of "supplements." Lope pulled off his leather hat and smeared a gnat off his face, and then wiped his hand on Squatlo's rump.

"You gonna' stay on out there a while?"

"Hard to say. Job's good; pay's better'n I can get here doing the same thing. Assuming I could find a job back here."

I cornered a minnow and studied on the problem of hooking him in the right place so he'd stay alive long enough to attract a barn door paper-mouth. At least I wanted it to look like that. We both knew I wasn't coming back.

Lope stretched.

"I'm thinkin' to build a gym in the shed back of the Scoot. Some of the old Club slide by now 'n then. New kids alla' time askin' to train. What's good to tell 'em?"

He was getting us onto familiar ground. I looked out across the lake with that old thousand yard—or thousand mile—stare and tried to say something not too stupid.

"Well, keep it simple, keep it basic, train for yourself, be realistic about your potential, don't pretend to be what you're not, but don't be afraid to reach for more, and don't think drugs'll get you something beyond your reach and . . ."

I looked up and Lope and Preacher Harley were both grinning at me. We all looked away and humphed and scratched and stared at our bobbers and tight lines.

Lope swacked the mutt with his hat. Squatlo had his nose in the chicken livers again.

"You know that ole Plymouth's still running? Took me three months to dry it out and find all the dead critters. Still runnin'."

Me too, maybe, I thought.

Lope pulled in a croaking mud-tom and twisted the hook out and slid the fish back in the water.

"Sounds like you when that bass served coffee." He turned and dug in his tackle box.

The moon moved overhead. There is no quiet like that of a late summer night on a Texas bass lake. Lope studied a mayfly on his rod tip.

"Heard from the redhead lately?"

"Yeah. She's O.K. Workin' for the state."

Lope lit a cigarette to keep the skeeters away. I shifted my butt off a sixteen-penny nailhead that had worked itself up out of the dock.

"I think I'll maybe try another country pretty soon. I've got some contacts I met at the Asia meets. There's things I want to see and stories to write."

No one said anything while Preacher Harley pumped up the lanterns and popped some more "supplements" for everybody before resuming his natural position. Lope looked at me from under his hat.

"That Yokohama Mama left her cleat marks, too, huh?"

Our eyes held in clear understanding. I knew how he meant it, and he knew he was one of a very few that could risk it. He'd left some things behind as well. Close as we were, that was just about the nearest it ever came to being out in the open.

Squatlo skooched over and laid his jaw on my knee. A loon called from the point across the slough. There was a rumbling behind us.

"As it says in the good book," Preacher Harley intoned, "To thine own self be true, and sitting well in order, propose to sail yet a little while beyond the sunset . . ."

Shakespeare and Tennyson as Scripture was too much even for Lope. He locked the Eastwood eyeball on the recumbent form.

"Preacher? You ever been baptised?"

"I, sir, am a theological intellectual, and such rituals . . . now . . . hey!"

Lope and I were rising together to share one last, best, great moment.

A s I said in the introduction, this book is not designed for complete beginners, but for people who have some training experience, whether five months or five decades. These courses are not designed for the great champions, but just for maybe 95% of everybody who trains.

I can't see you and don't know if you're a short-armed wonder, a natural physique type, a tall-and-lanky, an average Joe, a "hardgainer," or what. I don't know your level of progress or if your technique is lousy or if you've got the weights on backwards. That is why I've not had much of anything to say about "progression." Whether working with a fixed weight for more reps or doing a fixed number of reps and adding weight, trying to add five pounds a week to the big lifts or inching up with half-pound washers, it is *all* progression.

The pattern you choose depends on your goal.

For the most part, I recommend one to two warm-up sets and two or more work sets. Warm-ups should be just that, and not so strenuous as to drain energy from the work sets. The last several reps of a work set should be gut-busters that can be accomplished without breaking good form. But no matter what scheme you pursue, sooner or later you will level out, hit a wall, get stale or just flat become bored.

That is why cycling works so well. Nevertheless, I think any routine will become ineffective eventually, and a change of pace is required.

On the other hand, I believe no routine will do much good unless it is given a fair chance to produce results, and that means sticking to it for three or four months so results may be gauged. It may take two to four cycles over the course of a year to make an accurate appraisal. But I do not believe any routine, set-rep scheme or poundage progression, or for that matter, any theory of training, should be followed exclusively year in and out.

Where is it written that training cannot be fun? That is why over the years when I felt uninspired or bored, instead of a week layoff, I might just quit whatever I'd been on and devote a day to one-hand snatches, grip tricks or any movement I could think of that I hadn't tried lately. The resurgence of strongman and Highland Games competitions suggests that a lot of people are bored with living in the gym and doing the same old stuff. A little variety is good for your head and maintains your interest as well as being positive for your body.

Everybody please remember: General training to get bigger and stronger, and training specifically for and peaking toward competition of any kind is not the same thing. The courses in this book are for most people most of the time, except where I indicate otherwise, as in preparation for your first powerlifting meet or other specific purposes. They've all been proven in the gym.

The truth is that most people who like to train will never enter a contest. They're just gonna' feel good most of their life. The hope of this book is that more and more people will reach a point where they will compete, or if they never do, just get more satisfaction from their training whatever their goal.